ACKNOWLEDGEMENTS

The vast majority of the historical photographs reproduced herein come from three sources. I would like to thank each in turn. Firstly, I would like to extend my gratitude to the staff at the Royal Commission For Historical Monuments (RCHM), formerly known as the National Monuments Record, for their kind assistance and generous permission to reproduce their copyrighted material. Secondly, I am indebted to Ken Reedie and the Canterbury Museums for some of the fascinating pictures taken by the late Mr A. Moody, ARCA. Other photographs by Mr Moody came from a private source, to whom I am also grateful. Lastly, I would like to thank Messenger Group Newspapers for once more allowing me to plunder their vast archives.

Also, I would like to thank the following for providing textual material and historical information: Margaret Sparks, Clive Bowley, Jenny Wells, David Cousins, the Institute of Heraldic and Genealogical Studies and the Canterbury Archaeological Trust. A special vote of thanks must go to Anthony Swaine, whose revealing and sometimes shocking facts concerning the situation in Canterbury after the blitz have set the tone for this book.

The feature 'Canterbury Then and Now' appears regularly in the Kentish Gazette.

Photo of author (right) by Ruth Marshall.

Canterbury under fire. St George's Street looking east, as seen in the early hours of 1st June 1942. The Baedeker raid devastated large areas of Canterbury, including most of St George's Street. It also became the trigger for the drawing up of drastic plans to rebuild on a massive scale, the impact of which could have affected the entire city.

(Courtesy of Marks and Spencer PLC)

ST DUNSTAN'S STREET

St Dunstan's Street contains a wealth of beautiful timber framed buildings, constructed over nearly four centuries. The medieval Falstaff Inn on the street's north side is probably the best known. However, what is more impressive is the row of four large three-storey town houses, mainly from the 16th century, which can be found on the south side of the street.

The first of these, and part of the second, are pictured here in the autumn of 1942. The blast damage was caused by high explosive bombs which destroyed a number of buildings on the opposite side of the street around the junction with Station Road West. Some of these can be seen on the page opposite.

Fortunately, the buildings were considered important enough to be saved and were later superbly restored.

The first of the four buildings is the triple-gabled former Star Inn, seen in the centre of the old photograph. In the early 1940s the left hand bay was a draper's (No. 79), the centre bay was Flishers, the grocer (No. 78) and the right hand bay, part of the Rose and Crown public house.

The next building and partially visible to the right of the old picture is a quadruple-gabled structure. This encompassed the other half of the Rose and Crown (No. 76), Pettyfer the tobacconist (No. 75), Glover basket maker (No. 74) and St Dunstan's post office at No. 73.

The third building, at No. 72 St Dunstan's Street, has only the top storey jettied and with no gables fronting the street. It is not clear if it was originally constructed in this way, or if the gables and lower jetty disappeared during the process of 'Georgianisation'. In the early 1940s this building was the St Ninian's private school, run by Miss J. Scoons.

The fourth and final building is the famous House of Agnes (No. 71), another fine triple-gabled building, owned at the time by Colonel Bertrand Gostling, OBE.

It is hoped that these fine buildings will continue to grace St Dunstan's Street for many more centuries.

See CBB, Page 2

(Kent Messenger)

The south side of St Dunstan's Street today is as impressive as it always has been. The three-storey timber framed buildings are finely maintained and appear to have suffered no ill effects from the war damage. Many of the businesses found here in the 1940s have gone. However, the Rose and Crown public house is still to be found where it was fifty years ago.

(Paul Crampton)

This picture was taken in the opposite direction from those on page 2. It shows the devastation in the eastern corner of Station Road West with St Dunstan's Street. The main loss at this location was a five hundred year old timber framed building which had been moved here in 1906 by local builder Walter Cozens. This ancient structure originally stood in Upper Bridge Street and was threatened with demolition. However, keen historian Mr Cozens rescued it and moved it timber by timber to this site. The re-used building once housed a swimming bath, as well as Mr Cozens' own small museum on the upper floor. It ended its life as the Canterbury branch of the British Legion Club.

The damaged brick buildings dominating the picture are Nos. 6, 8 and 10 Station Road West. Numbers 6 and 8 were subsequently demolished, whilst No. 10 still survives today.
(Mr A. Moody)

Another, yet much closer, view of the former Star Inn building on the south side of St Dunstan's Street. This picture clearly shows the attractively carved corbels beneath the upper jetty.

The passageway to the left of the Rose and Crown once led to a collection of tiny cottages behind, known as Star Place. These tenements had all been abandoned by the end of the 1930s and were probably demolished at about the same time.

To the right of the picture can be seen three of the four bays of the next three-storey building. Over the years, each proprietor of the shops within the individual bays altered the appearance of his particular property. Some ended up with mathematical tiles, some with exposed timbers and some with plain plaster. Post-war restoration has given the structures a more unified appearance by using plain plaster-work throughout.

(Mr A. Moody)

No bombs fell on the city of Canterbury during 1943. The residents must have thought they had seen the last of the bombing. Sadly this was not the case, for there was to be one more raid on the city, albeit a half-hearted one. This occurred in the small hours of 22nd January 1944 and affected mainly the Westgate and St Dunstan's areas. The worst damage in the raid was sustained by the premises of motor engineers Barretts Ltd, situated on the corner of St Peter's Street and Pound Lane. The accompanying photograph was taken later on the same day, with the ruins still smouldering. The damaged building to the right, also belonging to Barretts, was then only seven years old when it was badly damaged in this conflagration. Ironically, it had replaced an earlier timber framed building which had itself been lost in a fire.

See CBB, Page 4 and BOC, Page 45 — Top
(Kent Messenger)

NORTHGATE

During the Baedeker raid on Canterbury a number of high explosive bombs were dropped at random over the north-east suburbs of the city. One particular bomb destroyed a group of houses at the western end of Union Street, near its junction with Northgate. The resultant blast was felt over a wider area and affected a group of late medieval cottages on the west side of Northgate. They lost all their windows and most of the roof tiles came away.

The old photograph was taken towards the end of 1942 and shows the same late medieval cottages in Northgate. However, the level of destruction seen here is quite severe and was not caused solely by the bombing in June earlier that year.

Another picture taken in July 1942 shows the same cottages with only the blast damage as described above. This photograph appears on page 5, with the cottages visible in the background. Otherwise they appeared to

be quite sound. So why, by the end of the same year, had they be partially dismantled to the state seen in the accompanying old pho graph?

The probable answer is that the cottages were victims of the unoffic de-roofing policy, as described on the introduction page of this boo

If true, then the removal of the roof from an 'unwanted' buildi would expose it to the elements and hasten its ruination. Then lat complete demolition could be justified.

The men at work in front of the cottages are not engaged in demoliti work, but are installing new traffic lights for the Northgate – Uni Street junction.

These ancient cottages were indeed subsequently swept away.

(Kent Messeng

The post-war buildings were put up from 1951 onwards. Like so mu early post war construction, they were built set back from the stre frontage. This would allow for later street widening, should that deemed necessary. These buildings, a garage and a shop, are current empty, and their future is uncertain. It is possible that they may soon demolished.

(Paul Crampto

As mentioned opposite, a high explosive bomb destroyed a number of cottages on the north side of Union Street, near its junction with Northgate. The picture shows the pile of debris that was once Nos. 1 to 4 Union Street. The badly damaged cottages at Nos. 5 to 7, just beyond the wreckage, were subsequently pulled down. Some blast damaged houses in Union Place can be seen on the left of the picture. Later, in the early 1950s, this large corner site was occupied by the garage and filling station of P.D. Tobin.

(Mr A. Moody: Courtesy Canterbury Museums)

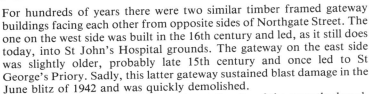

For hundreds of years there were two similar timber framed gateway buildings facing each other from opposite sides of Northgate Street. The one on the west side was built in the 16th century and led, as it still does today, into St John's Hospital grounds. The gateway on the east side was slightly older, probably late 15th century and once led to St George's Priory. Sadly, this latter gateway sustained blast damage in the June blitz of 1942 and was quickly demolished.

This Ministry of Works picture shows the site of the recently demolished Gateway. However, some timbers relating to its north wall still survive abutted to the next building. These adjacent cottages would also be demolished, despite their seemingly undamaged appearance. The photograph also includes, in the background, the late medieval cottages featured on page 4, but before their roofs were removed.

(© RCHM)

This picture was taken round the corner from the one above and shows some damaged buildings on the east side of Northgate Street. The date is 4th June 1942 and the occasion is the visit by the Duke of Kent to Canterbury. The jettied building behind the dignitaries is David Featherstone's fried fish shop. Next door is a public house, the Grapes Inn. These buildings were subsequently demolished and as shown in the picture above, the site later became part of Tobins Garage.

See BOC, Page 24

(Fisk-Moore)

The Northgate area was also a target for the raiders in October 1942, when a number of houses were flattened. This picture was taken at the far end of Northgate Street, just before the start of Sturry Road. It shows the flattened remains of the Jolly Gardeners' public house at No. 3 Northgate Street, which stood on the corner with Cold Harbour Lane. Further along can be seen a group of 17th century timber framed buildings. Nearest the camera is the general stores run by Edward Cottrell (No. 2 Northgate), then the tiny cottage of Mrs Izzard (No. 1), and finally the premises of the Sceptre Oil Company, lubricating oil merchants, at No. 1a Northgate.

These buildings soon became further victims of the demolition gangs. On the same site today, the Cold Harbour housing development can be found.

(Kent Messenger)

In the last ten years Stour Street has reverted to being a mainly residential area. Several new housing schemes have been built on sites once occupied by light industrial or retail businesses. Planning permission for residential redevelopment has also been granted for the Wiltshier Builders' yard, seen here, but this seems to be held up by the current recession.

(Paul Crampton)

STOUR STREET

The old photograph shows the surviving one of a pair of beautiful timber framed houses. The lost house was to the right of this one and was totally destroyed in a bomb blast (described on page 8). Further still to the right, another smaller timber framed building fronting Stour Street was also lost. This was the house and shop of Miss Kate Fuller, confectioner, and was situated near the junction with Beer Cart Lane, where the bomb fell.

The surviving house is pictured here on 18th June 1942, whilst awaiting a decision as to its ultimate fate. The top of the roof and the chimney stack to the left have been blasted away and the main frame was also slightly askew. However, I am assured by a conservation minded observer from the time, that it was perfectly capable of being repaired and restored.

Nevertheless, the final decision made was to demolish the survivor altogether. This was the fate of so many potentially salvageable buildings at the time. It could be said, quite understandably, that in a time of war there is no time, money or resources to worry about a few damaged timber framed buildings. Even making full allowance for this, demolition in many cases was unnecessary.

The photograph also shows debris still scattered along Stour Street, including some machinery and a large basket from Beasleys, further along on the opposite side of the street. The badly damaged building seen to the right and in the background is actually in Beer Cart Lane. It is one of three old cottages destroyed along that section of the lane.

See CBB, Page 10, Page 11 — Middle and TAN, Page 1   (© RCHM)

Opposite the timber framed house featured on page 6 there was an 18th century brick building occupied by the Weights and Measures Inspector. Behind and to the side of this was the famous Poor Priests' Hospital. The Weights and Measures building was destroyed by a large high explosive bomb that landed at the nearby Beer Cart Lane junction (see pages 8 and 9 for more details). Its remains are pictured here, with part of the aforementioned Poor Priests' Hospital visible behind.

Leaning against the ruined building can be seen the frame of an upper storey bay window and the front door, both belonging to the destroyed timber framed house opposite.

The remains of the Weights and Measures building were quickly cleared away and the area converted to hardstanding for vehicles. Today this area is planted out as an attractive herb garden.

See BOC, Page 18 — Middle   (© RCHM)

This is a superb study of the Poor Priests' Hospital as it existed in the summer of 1942. This beautiful building narrowly escaped destruction from the aforementioned HE bomb but sustained damage to the roof (see below). The majority of the fabric of the Poor Priests' dates from the last quarter of the 14th century. This makes its construction contemporary with that of the Westgate and the Cathedral Nave.

The section of the building to the right of the photograph was once the hospital chapel. The outline of the former chapel's great east window of soft Kentish Ragstone can clearly be seen.

In the late 16th century, when the lofty chapel had an upper floor inserted, the great east window was blocked up and two new windows inserted in accordance with the new layout.

Recent restoration has eliminated most traces of the 14th century chapel window, save a few oddly-placed stones marking its original outline.

(© RCHM)

This is an overall view of the area taken in August 1942. By this time, the remains of the Weights and Measures building to the left had gone. The surviving timber framed house, as featured on page 6, had also been demolished and its site was now serving as a hard standing area, currently containing one car and a cable drum. Repair work to the Poor Priests' Hospital had begun, as can be seen by the scaffolding erection against the south wall of the former chapel. It was discovered that the hospital's roof timbers had spread, due to the blast, and had to be hauled back into position.

At this time, occupation of the old Poor Priests' building was divided between the Canterbury Public Health Department and the St John Ambulance Brigade.

(© RCHM)

BEER CART LANE and STOUR STREET

The accompanying old picture shows clearly the sort of damage that a single high explosive bomb could do to the heart of a medieval city.

The unfortunate target was the junction of Beer Cart Lane and Stour Street. The resultant explosion not only damaged a number of ancient buildings, but also severed the mains services. This cut off vital water supplies to other parts of Canterbury and hampered the fire fighting efforts.

The damaged building in the centre of the photograph is part of the dye works of E. Beasley & Son Ltd. The far less damaged buildings to the left of it are also part of the same premises. The aforementioned badly damaged building was medieval and dated from the mid 14th century. It is sad to lose any old building to war, but especially one around 600 years old. The entire front section above the jetty had been

blown away. However, this comprised mainly a large early 19th centur Regency facade that extended above the first storey to conceal most c the hipped roof and its dormer window.

Despite its appearance, an early structural survey of the survivin fabric indicated the damage was not too severe and that the buildin could be restored. Architect Anthony Swaine designed a new frontag for the Beasley building that would have restored it to something like i pre-19th century appearance.

Sadly, the restoration plan was never adopted, because the cit planners envisaged a new roadway at this point that would cross th river to Black Griffin Lane.

See CBB, Page 11 — Top

(© RCHM

For many years Canterbury Cycle Mart occupied the new premises originally built for Beasleys. When they moved out, the building remained empty for a while and a planning application was made to redevelop the site for residential use. This appears to have been forgotten, for today the Harvey Centre can be found here. This is an indoor market of small shops of great variety and interest.

(Paul Crampton)

Another view of the damaged Beasleys buildings, this time taken from Beer Cart Lane. The picture is dated 18th June 1942, as is the one on the opposite page. The workmen are, no doubt, trying to restore the mains services, severed by the recent attack.

The building on the left is part of the premises of C & G Yeoman storage contractors, at No. 1 Beer Cart Lane. Today this corner site is occupied by the County Council four-storey office block.

(© RCHM)

This picture of the 14th century building was taken in July 1942. By this time the restoration plan had been abandoned and the decision made to cut the building down to size. The sloping front portion of the new corrugated iron roof is already in place. The damaged chimney stacks have also been dismantled. Soon, the remaining timbers of the ancient crown post roof would be removed and a flat corrugated iron roof installed. At this time, Beasley and Son were unable to use any part of their Stour Street premises. The notice on the door reads 'Beasleys still operating, enquire at Presbyterian Hall'.

This building continued to be used by Beasleys, in its reduced form, well into the 1960s. Then, together with the adjoining building, it finally gave way to newly constructed premises.

(© RCHM)

A fascinating study of the 14th-century roof timbers of the most seriously damaged of Beasleys buildings. The crown post roof support system can clearly be seen within the surviving loft space. The crown post itself is the main vertical timber, the horizontal members at the top are the collars and the small curved diagonal support timbers are the brackets. The common rafters behind the crown post have been completely stripped of tiles. All the roof timbers in front of the crown post were lost in the explosion.

(© RCHM)

This picture was taken at the top end of Beer Cart Lane and shows a group of interesting buildings which survived the blitz, on the lane's south side.

The pair of cottages on the right of this view and numbered 3a and 4 Beer Cart Lane, survive to this day as private dwellings. This is a considerable achievement, when so many other houses in this area have become offices. The next building at No. 5 is the combined premises of Ronald Parry's radio and battery services and the small motor garage run by Mr W.G. Hopkins. This building was demolished in the late 1960s, early 1970s, together with a number of others at the bottom end of Beer Cart Lane. A number of familiar buildings can also be seen further up and in Watling Street.

(Kent Messenger)

ST MARGARET'S STREET

It is now recognised that the Royal Fountain Hotel's claim to have been established in the 11th century is somewhat spurious!

The building itself was certainly nowhere near that old. Its external appearance would suggest that it was built in the late Georgian or Regency periods, with its stuccoed brick work and neo-classical influences. However, like so many of Canterbury's buildings, the facade hid a far older timber framed structure.

The Royal Fountain Hotel was so utterly destroyed in the Baedeker raid of 1st June 1942 (including all evidence of its true origin), that there was very little work for the demolition men to do, as the accompanying old photograph clearly shows.

This picture was taken on 4th June 1942 by Mr A. Moody, during clearing up operations. The centre of the devastation where the cloud of dust, or perhaps smoke, can be seen, marks the position of the front entrance to the former hotel's courtyard and stables behind. The word 'Partingtons' can be seen on a surviving billboard on what is left of the inner wall of the passage. Partingtons Billposting Ltd, advertisement contractors, operated from nearby Castle Street.

A number of other properties were destroyed by fire at various locations along the east side of St Margaret's Street. However, the west side of the street survived intact. Just as with Butchery Lane, to the north of the main street, St Margaret's Street became a fire break. Above all else, it was the fire fighters' task to stop the spread of the incendiary fires sweeping westwards. This task was aided by the north easterly wind, that carried both smoke and fire away from that part of the city that survived the holocaust. Moreover, at this particular location, it would seem likely that the firemen concentrated on saving and protecting St Margaret's Church opposite, probably at the cost of the hotel.

See CBB, Page 16 and BOC, Page 17 — Bottom (Mr A. Moody)

Throughout its forty-year life as a surface car park, this area was subject to several archaeological investigations. These uncovered a number of finds and remains relating to both the Roman and medieval periods. The present Marlowe Arcade development, on the St Margaret's Street side, started a trend towards 'pastiche' shop building that imitated a mixture of past architectural styles.

(Paul Crampton)

As stated opposite, the Royal Fountain Hotel was not the only blitz victim to be found on the east side of St Margaret's Street. This pile of collapsed bricks and timbers was once the premises of Frederick Matthews, house furnisher and cabinet maker, at No. 9 St Margaret's Street. The building, which had a magnificent late 17th or early 18th century staircase, was gutted by fire in the 1st June blitz, leaving only a charred and dangerously buckled shell. Demolition of the three-storey frontage had just taken place when this picture was taken.

The wall looming up to the left belongs to a large building, numbered 10 to 11, that contained several business premises including A.H. Amey and Son Ltd, blind manufacturers. This far less damaged building was also subsequently demolished.

See BOC, Page 18 — Top   (Mr A. Moody)

Initially, I had a certain amount of difficulty with a positive identification for this photograph. The original print was marked 'Freemasons Inn — St Margaret's St'. But why is it being referred to as Dirty Dicks? Perhaps this was the name of the Landlord? The 1940 Kelly's shows the proprietor as James Holloway and the 1949 directory lists Mr W.G. Baxter, so no help there.

The position was further confused by an advert for Slatters Hotel which can be seen in the picture, behind the bar. Part of the Slatters Hotel at No. 8 St Margaret's Street had been damaged in the blitz and later partially dismantled. Could this then be the Slatters Hotel?

Recently, a former patron of 'Dirty Dicks' confirmed that it was indeed the Freemasons Hotel, later demoted to the Freemasons Tavern, because many upper rooms had been destroyed. The remains of this damaged building lasted until final closure and demolition in 1965.

(Mr A. Moody)

he final photograph from the camera of Mr A. Moody is indeed a sad sight with a sad story. It shows the burnt ruins of the St Margaret's Stores, a grocer's shop run by Miss Cora Solley. The picture was taken from an upper storey of the building opposite, and has therefore not captured the surviving part of the ground floor shop front, the top of which has just crept into view.

In the mid 1930s Miss Solley took over from her father, I assume, Mr H. Solley. She remained as proprietor until her premises and adjacent home were destroyed in the blitz. Sadly, Miss Solley's beloved pet cats perished in the conflagration. The fire did not spread, as the buildings on either side survived.

See CBB, Page 17 — Middle   (Mr A. Moody)

WATLING STREET

The accompanying old photograph was taken in early 1943 and shows three fascinating buildings on the south side of Watling Street. They were spared in the blitz of Canterbury, but only just. All three suffered varying extents of incendiary fire damage to their roofs and upper storeys. Temporary repair work can clearly be seen on the two properties nearest the camera.

Of the three, the building on the extreme right does little to disguise the fact that it is a timber framed construction. This is the surgery at No. 25 Watling Street, occupied throughout the 1940s by Dr Gillies. The building dates from around 1500 and can therefore be considered as late medieval.

Next door at No. 26 is Latchmere House, which was constructed in 1620. Unlike the surgery building, its external appearance has changed radically over the years. Originally, Latchmere House may well have looked like the House of Agnes or the Star Inn in St Dunstan's Street (see pages 2 and 3). It was jettied between the ground and first floor and had a steep pitched roof instead of the rectangular second floor. The old roof may well have had two or three jettied gables facing the street, allow limited second floor living space.

In the Regency period, ie the 1820s, Latchmere House underwent some extensive alterations. A ground floor brick and stucco wall was made up to eliminate the first jetty and the second floor entirely rebuilt to the way we see it today. Also at this time, the front elevation was covered in mathematical tiles, which all fell away following the June blitz.

The building on the left at No. 27 Watling Street is probably contemporary with Latchmere House and has been subject to similar alterations over the years.

(© RCHM

It is fortunate that these three fine buildings were not lost in the blitz or the demolition crazed years after the war, when it was intended to demolish them for road widening. Watling Street today contains many fine buildings. Even those built in the post-war years were thoughtfully planned and have some merit. The only regret is that these fine town houses are no longer lived in, but used entirely as offices and business premises.

(Paul Crampton

This photograph was taken diagonally opposite the one on page 12 and shows a scene of devastation on the north side of Watling Street. The standing building, the side wall of which dominates this picture, is one of a pair of Jacobean style 17th century houses at No. 19 Watling Street. (No. 18 is hidden from view in this side-on angle.) Despite the fact the roof was gone, this structure, with its Dutch type gables and many chimney stacks, was still an impressive sight.

The double-gabled end wall once must have faced onto open ground, perhaps a garden area. Then later, when further buildings were erected very close to the Jacobean house, the three first floor side windows were blocked up. These early 19th century houses at Nos. 20 to 22 Watling Street were destroyed in the blitz. The remains of their stuccoed walls can be seen amidst the rubble.

See CBB, Page 18 (© RCHM)

Another view of one of the Jacobean houses, taken in July 1942. This time the frontage of No. 18 Watling Street can be seen to the left of the picture. The two Jacobean houses had been fire damaged, but a decision was taken to retain them (a surprising decision at a time when the demolition option was nearly always chosen). In fact, No. 19 continued to be used by Hawkins and Hawkins, analytical chemists, in the ground floor section, until 1953 when both houses were demolished.

In the centre of the picture is another much larger early 17th century town house (Nos. 16 and 17), which was built and occupied by the Mann family in 1625. By the 19th century the house had been divided in two, hence the street numbering. It was later re-united, when Mr Cecil Kingsford, Mr Robert Arrowsmith and Mr Norman Wightwick started their firm of solicitors here.

See CBB, Page 18 (© RCHM)

Watling Street suffered further blitz damage in the October 1942 raid, but on this occasion the target was the top section of the street. This particular photograph shows the demolished houses on the south side with soldiers trying to clear a path through the fallen debris. The farthest block of white rendered houses, Nos. 38 to 41 Watling Street stood between Marlowe Avenue and Watling Square. (The latter was a passage leading to some tiny tenements.) Standing next to Watling Square in this block is the Dane John Tavern.

The nearest block of red bricked houses was obviously the hardest hit. Of the eight houses in this section between Watling Square and the Dane John Gardens, seven were destroyed. Only No. 42 at the far end of this block was retained.

The buildings at Nos. 38 to 42 survived until the end of the 1940s, when they were demolished. Today the Watling Street surface car park can be found on this site.

(Kent Messenger)

In the early post-war plans for the rebuilding of Canterbury, Rose Lane was to become the grand Civic Way. This idea remained on the plans until the mid 1960s. Consequently, when Rose Lane was redeveloped from the 1950s onwards, it was greatly widened and re-aligned on a straighter route. These buildings near The Parade junction are mostly on the old street line, whereas those opposite are set far back as a result of road widening.

(Paul Crampton)

ROSE LANE

This dramatic scene of devastation was captured on the morning of 1st June 1942, probably not long after the conflagration had been quenched.

The gentleman picking his way through the rubble of Rose Lane could not have been aware of the precarious nature of the ruined structures in his path. The wrecked buildings on either side of the lane once belonged to two former hotel complexes.

The structure on the right once formed part of the Bakers Hotel which, as the visible notice will confirm, had relocated to Ivy Lane in the mid 1930s. The former hotel building then became the 'Parade Chambers'; premises comprising several businesses. This standing part is all that is left of the building. The main part fronting onto St George's Street, was timber framed and had burned to the ground.

The tottering edifices on the left side of Rose Lane once formed part of the Rose Hotel. This had recently ceased to trade. The brick and stucco facade nearest the camera had earlier belonged to the Rose Tap public house. It closed in 1919 and was absorbed into the Rose Hotel complex. In fact, the Rose Hotel comprised several different adjoining buildings of various ages and methods of construction. A brick facade had been constructed across The Parade elevation in the 18th century, to give the appearance of a single uniform building.

The Rose Hotel as a whole had no less than nine separate tiled pitched roofs and therefore plenty of crevices in which incendiary bombs could have lodged.

The ruined buildings were quickly cleared away and this part of Rose Lane opened out as it probably never had before. However, a sizeable portion of the ground floor elevation of the former Rose Tap was left and survived until the mid 1950s.

See CBB, Page 21 — Top See CBB, Page 21 — Top   (Kent Messenger)

This picture was taken shortly after the main raid of 1st June 1942 and shows the ruins of Rose Lane Central Garage, operated by Castle Motor Company. The garage was situated on the west side of the lane, a few yards away from St Mary Bredin Church.

The photographer, Mr A. Moody, is standing towards the rear of the premises and some 0 yards away from the Rose Lane frontage. It is unlikely that these vehicles will ever run again. Similar thoughts must be running through the mind of the man standing at the rear of the wrecked garage.

In late 1942 and 1943 the area was cleared of war damaged buildings and it was possible to see clearly through from Rose Lane to St Margaret's Street. In the mid to late 1940s 'East Kent' used to park buses on this area. Then, in the 1950s, Rose Lane was widened and the Marlowe car park extended to encompass this site.

(Mr A. Moody: Courtesy Canterbury Museums)

In the 1930s Rose Lane was an enclosed winding lane with a hotch potch of interesting buildings of different functions. For example, a walk from one end to the other would take you past thirteen cottages, a church, three garages, one pub (there had been two) and a miscellany of small businesses.

The raids of June and October 1942 irrecoverably changed the scene. Much of the area was flattened and only the south end near the junction with Watling Street was spared any serious damage. This picture was taken towards the south end of Rose Lane and shows the damage sustained in the daylight raid of 31st October 1942. On the right of the photograph is the ruined garage of E.J. Philpott Ltd. Further along can be seen the damaged premises of coach builders W.S. Williams & Son. Both premises later featured in the 1943 film 'A Canterbury Tale'.

See CBB, Page 21 — Bottom

(Kent Messenger)

1945, when this picture was taken, most of the blitzed damaged buildings along both sides of Rose Lane had been demolished. Further up Rose Lane and behind the cameraman, Williams Coach Builders and Philpott's Garage continued to trade in what remained of their premises.

This view is of the lower half of Rose Lane from Gravel Walk down to St George's Street and The Parade. On the left can be seen the premises of Wellworthy Piston Rings Ltd, one of the few buildings in Rose Lane to have escaped the blitz virtually intact. It finally gave way in the mid 1950s when this section of Rose Lane was straightened and widened. To the right of the picture can just be seen the 1939 rear extension of the Marks and Spencer building. In the middle distance on the left are the remains of the Rose Hotel including two windows from the ground floor Parade elevation.

(Canterbury City Council)

(Above) A famous cityscape taken at 11.00 a.m. on 1st June 1942. Smoke and steam from the damping down rises from the main area of destruction. The roofless Corn Exchange building can be seen, centre right. Beyond it is the burnt out St Mary Bredin Church. On the right is Butchery Lane with its right side intact and left side badly damaged in parts, but with all building frontages still standing at this time.

(Anthony Swaine)

(Below) A close up view of the Rose Lane area, during the second week of June 1942. In the foreground, demolition of the Corn Exchange is in progress. Opposite, the Rose Hotel was also being pulled down. On the left is the surviving Marks & Spencer shop and, behind it, the devastated Simon Langton schools. At the top of the picture the shell of St Mary Bredin's Church is still intact, as are other damaged and undamaged buildings in Rose Lane.

(Mr A. Moody)

(Above) A cityscape covering the same area as the view opposite, but about two weeks later. Clearing up operations in St George's Street are well in progress, although the lofty premises of Castle & Co. still stand. However, much demolition work has still not taken place between St George's Street and Burgate Street. The recently arrived barrage balloons were in the sky at the time this photograph was taken.

(Mr A. Moody: Courtesy Canterbury Museums)

(Below) August 1942 and a much changed scene. The demolition gangs had dealt with the Castle & Co. building and reduced the Corn Exchange down to its ground floor walls. In fact, St George's Street was virtually levelled by now. The Simon Langton barrage balloon is grounded in this view. To the right, the burnt out section of the school is being demolished. The Kentish Gazette printing works are to the left of Marks and Spencer.

(Fisk-Moore)

Traces of St Mary Bredin Church could still be found until 1952, when road widening finally swept them away. However, in 1980, foundations of both the medieval and Victorian churches were uncovered and recorded by the Canterbury Archaeological Trust. Today, a plaque showing the outline of both churches can be found on the wall of the Marlowe Arcade development now occupying the site.

(Paul Crampton)

ST MARY BREDIN CHURCH

St Mary Bredin Church in Rose Lane was built in 1868, to replace a smaller 13th century church, parts of which it incorporated. Therefore, it was only 74 years old when it was burnt out following an incendiary attack on 1st June 1942.

I avoid using the word 'destroyed', which I and other writers of Canterbury's recent history have used up until now, to describe the demise of St Mary Bredin. Clearly, the roof, spire, floor and pews were burnt away. However, a number of internal and external photographs, taken by the Ministry of Works in July and August 1942, indicate that the main structure, the shell, was still sound and well capable of restoration.

The Victorian church was constructed of brick as well as stone blocks recovered from the earlier building. The external walls were faced in flint with stone dressing on corners and buttresses. The old photograph of the inside of the church shows some of the building materials beneath where the plaster has fallen away. The picture shows the arcade of columns and arches that stood between the north aisle, where the photographer is standing, and the much taller central aisle. Beyond the arcade can be seen the western wall of the church and the large window at the west end of the central aisle.

Other photographs taken at the same time show that ancient internal monuments and memorials were transferred from the older church in 1868. A photograph of one such memorial can be found on the opposite page, together with more details.

Clearly, much more than an attractive Victorian church was lost when demolition workers were ordered to tear down St Mary Bredin Church in the autumn of 1942.

(© RCHM)

This external photograph of St Mary Bredin Church was taken from a short distance up Rose Lane and offers a splendid view of the gutted structure. The octagonal tower, now minus its spire, still looks sturdy, albeit somewhat charred on the topmost section. The tall gable end walls of the central aisle can be seen to the left and right of the tower. The much lower gables of the short south aisle area also visible on either side of the corrugated iron shed to the left of the picture.

The photograph was taken during the first four days of June 1942. This can be said with certainty, as on the night of 4th June the weather-boarded building on the right of the picture, belonging to L.L. Tyre Services Ltd, was destroyed in a minor raid.

The shell of St Mary Bredin survived until August of that year, but had been demolished by the end of October 1942. Compare this view with the one in the middle of page 15.

See CBB, Page 20 (Kent Messenger)

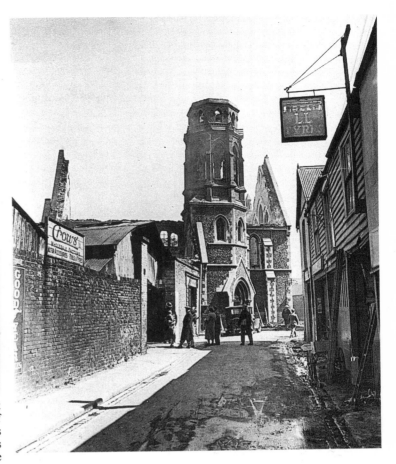

The two smaller pictures on this page together form a study of the west wall of St Mary Bredin Church. The upper view shows the section of wall to the left of the large central aisle window. The arcade of arches divides the central aisle from the south aisle, where the lancet windows can be seen. The south aisle was shorter than the others because of the existence of the base of the tower at its east end, through which one entered the church.

(© RCHM)

The above picture was taken from the central aisle and looks through another arcade of gothic style arches and columns into the north aisle. An unidentified tablet monument is visible on the wall, as is another in the upper view. Through the window of the north aisle can be seen the tower of St Margaret's Church in nearby St Margaret's Street (see page 10). This view had been made possible by the destruction of the Royal Fountain Hotel.

(© RCHM)

In August 1942 photographs were taken of two different early 17th century monuments, no doubt just prior to the church's demolition and (presumably) their destruction. The best of the two is featured here. This monument was identified by Edward Hasted in volume XI of his 'History of Kent', when it was then to be found within the preceding 13th century church. Hasted describes this handsome mural monument, on which are the figures of a man and a woman kneeling before a desk. The inscription is for William Mann who died in 1615. The other picture (not shown here), was of a badly damaged mural tablet, described by Hasted as being for Sir Christopher Mann, brother of William, who died in 1638. Both monuments include the Mann coat of arms, again from Hasted 'a chevron ermines, between three lions rampant, sable'.

The Mann family owned a large Jacobean house in nearby Watling Street, shown on page 13.

(© RCHM)

ST GEORGE'S STREET — NORTH WEST SECTION

Damage to the section of St George's Street on the north side, between Butchery Lane and Iron Bar Lane, was less severe than in any other part of the main street affected by the blitz.

Here, too, incendiary fire damage was serious, but had left three salvageable buildings in its wake. These were the premises of Montague Burton Ltd on the corner with Butchery Lane, Barclays Bank Ltd at 23 St George's Street, and in between them, the Corn Exchange and Longmarket building.

All three structures had suffered varying extents of fire damage, as can be seen in the accompanying photograph. All other buildings along this stretch were beyond help. Most notable of these was the National Provincial Bank building, the partly demolished facade of which can be seen to the right of the Corn Exchange in the old picture.

Of the survivors, Barclays was completely gutted, but all was not lost. The fate of the building is further told on page 21.

The Burton building had lost its roof and sustained fire damage to the first storey. Consequently, as with Barclays Bank, the upper storeys were removed and the undamaged ground floor retail area survived in use right up until late 1959.

The untimely and entirely unnecessary demolition of the beautiful facade of the Corn Exchange is considered on the opposite page. As in other parts of St George's Street, fascinating Roman remains were discovered here during the years between the blitz and the reconstruction. In 1945, just behind the Burton building, the famous Roman pavement was discovered. This was the mosaic floor of a room from a large Roman courtyard building. The find was not entirely unexpected, as Roman remains had come to light in the basement of Taylors the seed merchants, in the years before the war.

See CBB, Page 24 and TAN, Pages 32 and 33 (© RCHM)

In the mid 1950s both the new National Provincial and Barclays Banks were built on the sites of their blitzed predecessors. All the new buildings on the north side of St George's Street were individually designed and built. In context, the overall appearance of the street frontage is pleasing and stands up as the best example of early post war redevelopment in Canterbury.

(Paul Crampton)

This is the incredibly sad sight of the Corn Exchange pediment being knocked down with pick axes. This building had lost its roof and first floor timbers in the fire. A few of the iron roof supports had given way, but on the other hand, the basic brick structure was sound and undamaged. This picture clearly shows that the beautiful neo-classical frontage was still intact and with little evidence of even a scorch mark!

So why did this apparently salvageable building come to grief? It has been said that a radical new road plan for Canterbury had been drawn up within days of the Baedeker raid. This included a grand 'Civic Way'; a dual-carriageway following the line of Rose Lane and then continuing onto Burgate across the site of the damaged Corn Exchange building.

Demolition of the surviving structure started during the second week of June 1942, as seen in the accompanying picture. The rest of the upper storey walls were pulled down by crane. The ground floor walls were retained to provide an enclosed area where temporary shops could be erected prior to the construction of the Civic Way.

See CBB, Page 25 — Top, BOC — Front Cover and TAN, Pages 16 & 17
(Mr A. Moody)

The picture below shows all that remains of the once-beautiful building at No. 25 St George's Street. The chimney and walls seen here once formed part of the rear of this structure. This building encompassed the National Provincial Bank Ltd, a firm of auctioneers and a private flat occupied by Miss Margaret Babington OBE, steward of The Friends of Canterbury Cathedral. Part of the Corn Exchange building can be seen on the left, and part of Barclays Bank to the right.

See CBB, Page 25 — Bottom
(Mr A. Moody)

The photograph above was taken during the second week of June 1942 and in the opposite direction to the picture on page 20. By this time the facade of the National Provincial Bank had been completely demolished, leaving just a fragment against the Corn Exchange building. The substantial structures of both the Corn Exchange and Barclays Bank buildings can be seen to good advantage at this angle. However, demolition gangs would soon set to work on both of them.

See BOC, Page 14 — Middle
(Mr A. Moody)

The pre-war Barclays Bank building was not as old as it first appeared. It was constructed in the 1920s, with a mock double-jettied timber framed frontage. In fact, whether this was intentional or not, it bore a resemblance to the 17th century building in Palace Street known as the King's School Tuck Shop. As was mentioned opposite, Barclays Bank suffered quite severe fire damage, but part of the shell was considered strong enough to be re-used. Consequently, the upper storeys were demolished and the ground floor section repaired for continued use as a bank. In the meantime Barclays customers were asked to use Lloyds Bank in the High Street.

Whilst this was going on the National Provincial Bank built a new single-storey bank on the site of their demolished premises, a few yards along from Barclays. Both bank buildings lasted in this form until 1953.

See CBB, Page 29 — Left
(Kent Messenger)

21

ST GEORGE'S STREET — SOUTH WEST SECTION

The Simon Langton Schools were hidden behind the south-west section of St George's Street, on a site once occupied by the Augustinian or Austin Whitefriars. The original school buildings were concentrated in the north-west quadrant of the Whitefriars site, and almost adjacent to the St George's Street shops. The rest of the former monastic site was laid out for recreational purposes, such as tennis courts, playgrounds and gardens.

At time went by, each school expanded in size and new extension buildings were put up. Those for the girls' school were, in the main, constructed around the existing buildings. However, the extension buildings for the boys strayed into the southern parts of the site, and occupied the street frontages of Gravel Walk and St George's Lane.

Consequently, following the blitz of Canterbury which was concentrated on and around St George's Street, some 90% of the girls' school buildings were destroyed, whilst about 50% of the boys' school perished. The surviving boys' school buildings were those on the south of the site and away from the main conflagration.

The old photograph featured here shows part of the 10% of the girls' school which had survived. The roof was repaired and the building taken over by the boys' school. By this time, the Simon Langton Girls' School had transferred to Stone House (now St Martin's Hospital). To the surviving 50% of the boys' school and 10% of the former girls' school were added prefabricated buildings. On this basis, the Simon Langton Boys' School remained at Whitefriars for another 17 years.

The old building seen here was finally demolished in June and July of 1960, a few months after the boys' school had relocated to their new premises at Nackington.

See CBB, Page 27 — Middle (Mr A. Moody)

The current picture shows the rear of the arcade of shops built along the south side of St George's Street in 1952 and 1954. This did not interfere with the Simon Langton Boys' School which remained here until late 1959. The Whitefriars site then became a huge surface car park for ten years. Even at this time, a flint wall belonging to the old Whitefriars could still be found.

(Paul Crampton)

This view was taken during the morning of 1st June 1942 from halfway along St George's Street and looks towards The Parade section of the main street. Firemen, damping down the scorched rubble on the street's north side, are creating columns of grey-coloured smoke and steam. A much larger section of the south side of St George's Street can be seen on the left of the picture. Where now there are only smoking ruins, once stood the premises of well known businesses such as E. Bing and Son, Singer Sewing Machine Co. Ltd, Macfisheries and the office of Kent County Newspapers Ltd, who published the Kentish Gazette.

The Marks and Spencer building stands up proudly and undamaged. It was built in 1930, with a frontage that mirrored the neo-classical style of the Corn Exchange building opposite. Just on the other side of Marks and Spencer can be seen the gutted remains of the Canterbury Club.

(Kent Messenger)

As was mentioned in the above caption, the premises of the Singer Sewing Machine Co. (at No. 40 St George's Street), were utterly destroyed in the June blitz. Situated behind this shop could be found the East Kent and Canterbury Conservative Club and this can be seen in the accompanying picture. This single-storey building was totally gutted and presented a very sorry spectacle when photographed by the Ministry of Works in July 1942.

Adjacent to this was a similar single-storey building that housed the printing press of the Kentish Gazette and the Kent Herald newspapers. Luckily, this escaped the conflagration and the presses were soon rolling again. On the negative side, the newspapers' office building in front, at No. 39 St George's Street, was destroyed.

The Conservative Club building was soon demolished except for the right hand party wall shared with the newspaper printing press building.

(© RCHM)

This panoramic view of St George's Street was taken in the first half of July 1942. The photographer was standing on the rear section of the roof of Marks and Spencer, this being the only shop building in the street to escape unscathed. The intact low roof in the foreground belongs to the aforementioned Kentish Gazette printing press building, which also had a lucky escape. The site of their former office building on the street frontage is still covered in demolition rubble. By the time the picture was taken, the clearance of blitz damaged property on both sides of the street was well advanced. Chestnut paling fences were being erected, many of which would remain in place for nearly ten more years.

Kent County Newspapers did not miss an edition of the Gazette and had soon erected two wooden sheds, adjacent to their surviving press building, to act as temporary offices. The Kentish Gazette continued to be produced from these premises until early 1954.

(Kent Messenger)

ST GEORGE'S STREET — NORTH EAST SECTION

Following the Baedeker raid of 1st June 1942, no salvageable buildings could be found on the north side of St George's Street between Iron Bar Lane and Canterbury Lane. The intense incendiary fires had utterly destroyed all timber framed buildings along this stretch, leaving just scorched and fragile brick party walls and chimney stacks.

These tottering remains were the first priority for the demolition gangs, who set to work virtually as soon as the fires had been quenched.

The old photograph was taken during the first week of June 1942, by Mr A. Moody of the Canterbury School of Arts and Crafts. It shows the early demolition and clearing up process in operation. The three men in the centre foreground have just secured a chain around the wall and chimney stack on the left. This wall once divided the premises of Wards Confectioners at No. 15 St George's Street from Pettit the tobacconists

at No. 14. A large section of the wall with a gable end had already been taken down and the crane would shortly make light work of the rest of it.

Beyond the crane can be seen the scorched yet intact tower of St George's Church, as can the facade of the White Lion public house next to it.

Initially, demolished brick rubble was allowed to fill the many cellars, virtually where the walls had fallen. However, it was soon realised that this process might be concealing unexploded bombs. Therefore the rubble had to be painstakingly removed, and subsequently dumped into the 120 foot wide, four-ton bomb crater in Burgate Street.
See CBB, Page 28 & Page 29 — Top Right, and BOC, Page 28 — Bottom (Mr A. Moody: Courtesy Canterbury Museums)

The new shop buildings along this stretch were constructed between 1951 and 1954. The very first of these was Woolworths, which opened to huge crowds in the summer of 1952. The last was the David Greig building next to the junction with Canterbury Lane. At the time David Greig won an award for its rather radical yet impressive design. It is currently being used by W.H. Smith whilst their premises are being refurbished.

(Paul Crampton)

This picture was taken only a few seconds after the one on page 24. The doomed party wall now crashes to the ground while the demolition workers look on. Any standing walls near to street frontages were the first to be dealt with. Then the fallen rubble could be cleared and the thoroughfares opened. Any subsequent demolition would therefore not interfere with the traffic or pedestrians. Just beyond the crane can be seen the ruins of the once large premises of David Greig Ltd at Nos. 12 and 13 St George's Street. This too would soon attract the attention of the demolition crane, as would the burnt out shell of the White Lion public house further along and on the other side of the Canterbury Lane junction. St George's Church, in the background, would also not completely escape this process.
See CBB, Pages 28 & 29 — Top Right, and BOC, Page 28 — Bottom
(Mr A. Moody: Courtesy Canterbury Museums)

This photograph dates from the end of June 1942, when all lofty walls adjacent to St George's Street had already been reduced to piles of rubble. The long wall running across the middle of the picture is the same one so dramatically featured in the top picture, but now greatly reduced in height. It was at about this time that someone realised that allowing the demolition rubble to fill the open cellars of bombed buildings was not such a good idea after all. However, very few, if any, unexploded bombs were discovered when the rubble was moved out again.

A confusing collection of chimneys and gables is still standing back from the street frontage. Just beyond these can be seen the surviving bakery building of Arthur Loyns in Canterbury Lane. The trucks in St George's Street belong to Messrs C. & G. Yeoman, a Canterbury firm whose vehicles were much in evidence during the clearing up operation.

(Fisk-Moore)

A breathtaking study of the Cathedral and one that can also be found on the front cover of this book. It was taken during the winter of 1942 through to 1943, by which time the clearance of blitz damaged buildings in the central area was nearly complete. As mentioned opposite, all the rubble originally allowed to fill the cellars was removed and taken to the large bomb crater on the north side of Burgate Street.

In the immediate foreground can be seen some Simon Langton schoolboys who are walking along what was once a narrow passage between buildings, at the street end of which was Whitefriars Gate. The route of Iron Bar Lane can also be traced from St George's Street to Burgate Street. Here, the only buildings left are two small brick garages. The surviving buildings in Burgate can clearly be seen, albeit still with shattered windows and missing roof tiles.
See CBB — Front Cover   (Kent Messenger)

ST GEORGE'S STREET — SOUTH EAST SECTION

Before 1942 the south side of St George's Street comprised a continuous succession of buildings, constructed over a period of six centuries.

The June blitz of that year changed all that, as the accompanying old photograph dramatically illustrates. It was taken in late morning on 1st June 1942, when the firemen were damping down the last of the smouldering ruins of Canterbury. However, these firemen appear to be more interested in the cameraman than the ruinous facade in front of them. The three 'Romanesque' arches made of brick and stucco once formed part of the frontage of No. 49 St George's Street. These were the premises of the publishers of the Kentish Observer & Canterbury Chronicle.

The most interesting standing structure in this picture can be seen between the two pairs of firemen. It is the famous Whitefriars Gateway, lately used for access to the Simon Langton Girls' School. Up until now, it has generally been accepted by most people that the gateway had been destroyed in the blitz of Canterbury, but that was not the case. It now seems that the Whitefriars Gateway, that had been restored only a few years before, was demolished along with the ruinous shop frontages such as that of the Kentish Observer building.

Another interesting structure is the one visible beyond the gateway. This narrow Victorian building, standing some five storeys tall, was the premises of Castle & Co. Ltd, wine merchants, at No. 43 St George's Street. It had been completely burnt out but the solid shell stood for a number of weeks after the blitz, probably because its demolition was a daunting and difficult task.

See CBB, Page 29 — Bottom (© RCHM)

This is the arcade of shops (then known as Raveseft development No. 1), the rear of which can be seen on page 22. The sign denoting the entrance to the Whitefriars Shopping Centre is at exactly the spot where the Whitefriars Gate once stood. In the 1950s the passage through the new shops was used to gain access to the Simon Langton School, just as the pre-war passage once had been.

(Paul Crampton)

A fascinating study of the south-west section of St George's Street as it appeared on the morning of 1st June 1942. The utter devastation wrought to the once superb buildings from the St George's Lane junction down to Whitefriars Gate and beyond was perhaps even more severe than on the north side of the street. On the far left, where once stood the Coach and Horses public house, there is now only a pile of rubble. Next to it are the two party walls and steel joist once belonging to Woolworths at No. 54 St George's Street. Beyond that, the lower steel joist is all that is left of the attractive 15th century timber framed shop building of William Pollard, the jeweller (No. 53).

Further down can be seen further wrecked shops, Whitefriars Gate and the lofty ruins of the Castle and Co. wine merchants' building still standing defiantly. These burnt out premises with the twelve-flued chimney stack dominated the south side of St George's Street, even more so in the days after the blitz.

See CBB, Page 33 — Top Left and Right

(© RCHM)

This picture of the middle section of St George's Street was taken quite early on the morning of 1st June, certainly some hours before the pictures above and on the page opposite. The three-storey shop frontage in the centre of this view would partially collapse into the street between this photograph being taken and the one on page 26. (Closer inspection will reveal ominous cracks in the fire-baked masonry at the top.) Before the blitz this building was the premises of Fleming, Reid & Co. Ltd's wool stores, at No. 48 St George's Street. On the same side of the street, the Whitefriars Gate and Castle wine merchants' building are obscured by columns of steam from the damping down process.

On the north side of the street (right of the picture) can be seen the party wall, subject of the dramatic demolition sequence on pages 24 and 25.

(Kent Messenger)

By the fourth week of June 1942, when this photograph was taken, the demolition and clearance on both sides of St George's Street was nearly complete. In the weeks to come, any remaining wall fragments would be taken down to ground level, but for the moment it is possible to identify where former buildings once stood. This view was taken in the opposite direction to the ones above, which puts the south side of St George's Street on the right of the picture. The large jagged wall fragment in the foreground is all that is left of the five-storey Castle and Co. wine merchants' building. Beyond it can be seen the white line of the Whitefriars passage, at right angles to St George's Street. Nearest the street end, a stump of the demolished Whitefriars Gate is just visible.

Further along the south side, the clearance operation has removed most traces of the ruins that appear in the above pictures. At the far end to the right can be seen the burnt out Sun Buildings on the St George's Terrace slope.

See BOC, Page 28 — Bottom

(Fisk-Moore)

ST GEORGE'S CHURCH

Recently, much has been written about the history of the parish church of St George the Martyr. I do not intend to repeat this here. However, the archaeological investigation of the church site in 1991, together with a detailed study of the fabric of the standing tower, has changed some long held beliefs as to the age of the church and tower. Therefore, I will concentrate merely on those facts that now render some of my feature on page 30 of 'Canterbury Before The Blitz' out of date.

The tower is now thought to be almost entirely of 15th century date, rather than mostly 12th century with a 15th century top section, as originally thought. It now seems that the 15th century tower was built inside a 12th century extension to the nave. The Norman doorway and lower section of the west wall of the tower were part of the west wall of the nave for nearly three hundred years, before the tower was built inside it and bonded to the earlier fabric.

As I am sure everyone is already aware, St George's Church was burnt out as a result of the Baedeker raid of 1st June 1942. The accompanying photograph is a fine study of the surviving shell of the church, taken shortly after the blitz, probably on 2nd June 1942. The church is often described as having been destroyed in the night of the blitz. Contemporary photographs and accounts would seem to indicate that the standing shell of St George's was sound and, therefore, capable of restoration.

The following four page feature on St George's Church contains ten pictures, taken both inside and outside of the building at various times throughout June and July 1942. Many of these are being published for the first time. The accompanying text tells of the amazing story of these remains during that period.

For a more detailed history of the church, I would heartily recommend the article by Tim Tatton-Brown in the 15th Annual Report of the Canterbury Archaeological Trust.

See CBB, Page 30 See CBB, Page 30   (© RCHM)

The fate of St George's tower was in the balance right up until 1952, when the decision was taken to restore it. Even then there was a row as to who would pay for this work to be done. The first arcade of shops (Ravenseft development No. 2), was built round the tower in 1955. These were demolished in late 1990 and at the time of writing the new clocktower scheme was nearing completion.

(Paul Crampton)

This amazing photograph was taken even earlier than the one on page 28. The cameraman has captured a busy scene at about midday on 1st June 1942. The negative is damaged but is certainly worth reproducing here. By this time, the main conflagration had been quenched and, as can be seen, firemen, workmen and military personnel now have time to survey the surrounding devastation. The rubble in the immediate foreground is completely concealing the narrow St George's Lane junction. It probably fell from the brick frontages of Jay's Furnishing stores and the chimneys of the Coach and Horses public house (on either side of this junction), both of which were otherwise mainly timber framed and therefore utterly destroyed.

St George's looks remarkably intact, save for the missing nave roof and spire atop the tower. Scorch marks can also be detected in the flint work above the belfry window, testament to the conflagration started less than 12 hours before.

See CBB, Back Cover (Kent Messenger)

Moving forward in time a few days to Thursday 4th June 1942 and the day when the Duke of Kent paid a visit to Canterbury, to survey the devastation and raise the morale of its citizens.

Three photographers accompanied the royal party on their trip around the city. They were Mr W. Fisk-Moore (see 'The Blitz Of Canterbury', pages 21 to 24), Mr A. Moody (see this volume pages 58 and 59) and a photographer from the Kent Messenger. The last mentioned anonymous gentleman was responsible for this view of the royal party and local dignitaries outside the church. The Duke can be seen on the right of the party, standing next to the Rector of St George's, Geoffrey Keable. The Reverend Mr Keable held the position of Rector from 1933 until 1946, although the parish of St George's existed for a few years longer. At the time of writing, Geoffrey Keable is still alive, aged 92. He attended the ceremony of commemoration and reconciliation held in Canterbury during the first week of June 1992.

(Kent Messenger)

This picture was taken during the third week of June 1942, by which time the clearance of blitz damaged buildings in the vicinity of St George's Church was well advanced. The Kent Messenger photographer is standing in the ruins of the Sun Buildings on St George's Terrace from where many similar shots were taken throughout the 1940s.

In the immediate foreground can be seen a demolition workers' lorry and compressor unit, parked in St George's Lane. Just beyond these are the remains of the outbuildings and yard wall that were once situated behind the Coach and Horses. The pub at No. 56 St George's Street stood on the western corner of the junction with St George's Lane.

The mutilated St George's Church dominates the scene, the story of which is further told on pages 30 and 31. Next to the church are the ground floor remains of the White Lion public house, its substantial brick shell having been mostly demolished in the previous week. At the far end of the street can be seen the Corn Exchange building, with demolition in an advanced state.

See CBB, Page 33 — Bottom, and BOC, Page 32 — Middle (Kent Messenger)

This page contains three rarely seen views of the inside of St George's Church taken in the weeks following the blitz of Canterbury. The first picture was taken in the first few days of June 1942. The photographer is standing in the south aisle, with the tower behind him. He is looking through an arcade of arches and columns into the new nave and thence through another row of arches into the Victorian north aisle. At the end of the nave is the chancel, also Victorian, wherein can be seen the altar and decorated reredos with its central crucifix.

Against the first column in the arcade between the nave and the north aisle is a stone base with very short support columns. This may have been the stone base of the wooden pulpit. The door on the left led from the north aisle into a porch and then out into the graveyard. Another door, visible in the east wall of the north aisle, led to a recently built vestry.

See CBB, Page 31 — Bottom   (© RCHM)

Another internal picture, taken at about the same time as the view above. As can be seen in both photographs, the floor of the church is covered in shattered roof tiles and sad fragments of internal church 'furniture'. The tower is the main subject of this shot. As was mentioned on page 28, it is now thought that the tower is substantially of 15th century origin. However, the crenellated parapet was added in the late 18th century, at about the same time as the stair turret was removed and the needle spire transferred to the main tower.

On 12th June 1942 local architect and then war damage assessor, Anthony Swaine, made some detailed and measured drawings of the standing fabric of the church. He found the tower and the walls of the body of the church to be in good order and perfectly capable of complete restoration. Moreover, most of the glass in the north wall of the church was still intact. However, events were soon to take some interesting turns.

(© RCHM)

Sometime between 13th and 17th June 1942 demolition gangs moved in to pull the church down. A concerned citizen, whom I have not been able to identify, at once telephoned Sir Albert Richardson of the Ancient Monuments Society. He came down to Canterbury straight away, presumably on the next available train, and exerted his influence to stop the demolition work. At this time, the tower was thought to date from the 12th century, and its loss would have been of great concern to the Ancient Monuments Society as well as to local historians.

Sadly though, by the time Sir Albert Richardson could intervene, much damage had already been done. This photograph, taken by the Ministry of Works on 18th June 1942, shows that a substantial amount of the top of the tower had been pulled down.

The picture also shows that by this time the elaborate brick chimney stacks of the burnt out White Lion public house, next to the church, had also been demolished.

(© RCHM)

This external view was taken on 18th June 1942, by the Ministry of Works. It is clear that the demolition of the tower had reached the belfry stage and had entirely removed the 18th century crenellated parapet. A large section had also been taken out of the south wall of the old nave (that became the south aisle after 1872). It is unclear whether this was caused by masonry falling from the tower or if it was separate demolition work. The affected part of the south wall was much thicker than the rest of it, in that it was where the old staircase to the belfry started. The blocked up doorway to this staircase can be seen in the internal pictures at the bottom of the opposite page. Presumably, the staircase then crossed into the turret once situated at the external south-west angle of the main tower.

The flag of St George and of England can be seen hanging from the street post in front of the body of the church.   (© RCHM)

The intervention by Sir Albert Richardson certainly prompted a change of heart by the local authorities. Evidently, he really 'kicked up a stink'. By 2nd July 1942, when this picture was taken, scaffolding was being erected around the tower. This was, in part, to protect the fabric from any further deterioration and also to facilitate rebuilding the belfry section of the tower, demolished about two weeks before. Sadly though, it would appear that a further large section of the south wall of the church had been demolished or had collapsed. Collapse is likely, as this ancient wall must have been severely weakened by the earlier demolition work.

By this time virtually all trace of the White Lion, to the left of the church tower, had been removed. Gone too was the burnt out shell of the Old Rectory that once stood immediately to the north of the church.
(© RCHM)

The date is now 30th July 1942. The scaffolding erection is complete and the enforced rebuilding is well in hand. This work involved completely bricking up the belfry windows to add strength and to restore the tower to the original height of the stone course below the parapet. Nothing more would be done until the more comprehensive restoration of the tower carried out in 1953 and 1954.

So why was there an attempt to demolish the church in the first place? One version of the events states that the intention was merely to remove the 'unsafe' fire damaged part of the tower and then rebuild it anyway. This may be valid and should be taken into account. However, given the preference for demolition rather than restoration at that time, it would seem more likely that the burnt out church was considered to be just another damaged building to be cleared away. After all, the complete demolition of St George's Church would have allowed for the straightening out of an awkward bend in the main street, a point the planners cannot have overlooked.
(© RCHM)

(Above) The St George's and Whitefriars area of the city seen during the second week of June 1942. To the right is the Castle & Co. wine merchants' building. On the left is St George's Church, just prior to the demolition of the top of the tower. In the middle distance can be seen the oast house and cottages of St George's Lane. Running across the top of the picture is the lengthy row of burnt out houses on the city wall along St George's Terrace.   (Mr A. Moody)

This view looks due east towards St Augustine's Abbey and the huge void beyond, later to be filled with the buildings of Christ Church College. In the foreground is Lady Wootton's Green, with a good view of the north side. Behind the Georgian house, which encompasses the Almonry Chapel ruins, can be seen a long building, formerly the Almonry Hall. It was later demolished, despite showing only minor damage.   (Mr A. Moody)

(Above) Cityscape south east, looking across the eastern arm of Burgate Street towards Burgate Lane, Lower Bridge Street and St George's Place beyond. It is the second week of June 1942 and very little demolition work has taken place in this area. Of special interest are the rarely photographed buildings in Lower Bridge Street on either side of the junction with Ivy Lane. These appear to have sustained little or no damage. (Mr A. Moody)

(Below) Cityscape south east in August 1942. The apparently undamaged buildings in Lower Bridge Street have all but disappeared. The burnt out houses in St George's Place have been demolished as has the ruin of Starrs House in the bottom left hand corner of the picture. Other demolition victims include Nos. 2 and 3 St George's Gate. The buildings of the former St George's Primary School can be seen centre right amongst a group of trees. (Fisk-Moore)

Today St George's Lane bears no relation to the lane that existed in the 1940s. Then, it extended only as far as Gravel Walk and was little more than seven feet wide. It became a dual-carriageway in 1962, at the same time as the Riceman's Department store was built. The extension through to Watling Street came in 1969, when the adjacent multi-storey car park was constructed.

(Paul Crampton)

ST GEORGE'S LANE

This is one of my favourite then and now comparisons. The old photograph was taken by the Ministry of Works in July 1942 and shows the then surviving buildings along the east side of St George's Lane.

In the immediate foreground is the end wall of No. 9 St George's Lane, and all that remains of the properties formerly at Nos.9 to 12 St George's Lane. Then, beyond a narrow passage, is the large oast house belonging to Cooper and Wacher — the hop merchants. The oast sustained minor blast damage at the rear during the raids of the previous month. Other than that, it was structurally sound.

Next in the sequence are the rear garden walls of Nos. 13 and 14 St George's Terrace. These were the only two houses on the terrace whose gardens extended right down to St George's Lane. The remaining gardens of St George's Terrace extended only as far as Sheepshank Alley, which ran behind the properties of St George's Lane.

Beyond the gardens are the terraced houses of Nos. 4 to 8 St George's Lane. No. 8, nearest the camera, was at right angles to the other cottages. There was a covered walkway through to Sheepshank Alley between Nos. 5 and 6. The cottages had not completely escaped damage in the June raids. No. 5 was burnt out, and there was also minor fire damage to the roofs of Nos. 4 and 6.

Unfortunately, the cottages and oast house were not destined to survive for long. In 1943 the damaged cottages at Nos. 4 to 6 were demolished and, sadly, the old oast house was also pulled down. Nos. 7 and 8 St George's Lane lasted until the early 1950s, when they too were finally demolished to make way for the new bus station.

(© RCHM)

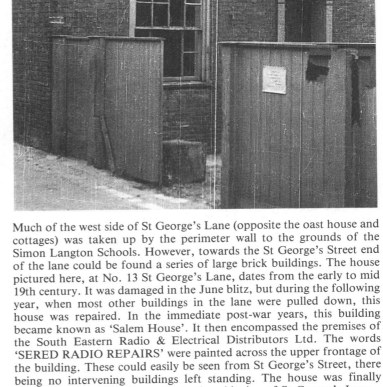

A close up study of the front of the oast house in St George's Lane. Former resident of No. 8, Jenny Wells (née Flint), remembers the old St George's Lane and, in particular, the old oast house near their cottage. The oast remained in deep sleep until hop picking time each year, when it would burst into life. Then, the two furnaces beneath the drying towers at the rear would be lit and the oast house start to take delivery of bulging sacks of fresh hops. These would be hauled up by pulley, from the horse-driven cart in the lane at the front, to the top opening, visible in this picture.

The kindly hop drying men would allow the local children to help in this process. Later the dried hops would be pressed, sewn into hop pockets and taken away for storage. Sadly, when the oast house was photographed here, perhaps for the last time, it could no longer play host to this charming annual ritual.

(© RCHM)

Much of the west side of St George's Lane (opposite the oast house and cottages) was taken up by the perimeter wall to the grounds of the Simon Langton Schools. However, towards the St George's Street end of the lane could be found a series of large brick buildings. The house pictured here, at No. 13 St George's Lane, dates from the early to mid 19th century. It was damaged in the June blitz, but during the following year, when most other buildings in the lane were pulled down, this house was repaired. In the immediate post-war years, this building became known as 'Salem House'. It then encompassed the premises of the South Eastern Radio & Electrical Distributors Ltd. The words 'SERED RADIO REPAIRS' were painted across the upper frontage of the building. These could easily be seen from St George's Street, there being no intervening buildings left standing. The house was finally pulled down in 1960, just prior to the widening of St George's Lane.

See CBB, Page 32 (© RCHM)

This general view of St George's Lane includes buildings on both sides and was taken in the opposite direction to the picture on page 34. The cottages at Nos. 4 to 8 St George's Lane can be seen to good advantage, as can the entrance to the rear passageway, right in the middle of the picture. The massive structure of the oast house is furthest from the camera. (A rear view of this building can be seen on page 39.) Right at the far end of the lane can just be seen some outbuildings, associated with the large house up on St George's Terrace, known as 'Terrace House'.

To the right of the picture are the ruins of the printing works of J.A. Jennings Ltd. Beyond them can be seen the edge of the house at No. 13, pictured above. The remains of the printing works would shortly be demolished. The other buildings in St George's Lane would have to wait until 1943 before their fate was known. As has already been mentioned, only the houses at Nos. 7, 8 and 13 survived the demolition purge of that year.

See CBB, Page 32 (© RCHM)

ST GEORGE'S GATE

The devastation caused by the Baedeker raid to the top end of the main street is all too evident in this dramatic photograph, taken from St George's crossroads. An earlier then and now feature showed a pre-war picture taken from near this spot and makes a very interesting comparison.

The blitz photograph was taken on 4th June 1942, the day the Duke of Kent visited the city. The police have erected a 'no-entry' sign, no doubt in preparation for the royal walk along the devastated St George's Street.

The short stretch of main street in the immediate foreground is St George's Gate. Of the five shops which once stood on the right, there are now only three. The furthest two, Nos. 4 and 5 St George's Gate, had burnt to the ground only four days before.

Of the survivors, Nos. 2 and 3 had serious fire damage and would shortly be demolished. However, the premises of E. & L. Bates, the gun-smiths, would soon reopen in a wooden shed on the site of their demolished shop. Only Pettit & Sons — tobacconists, visible on the extreme right of the picture, survived and lasted until the construction of St George's roundabout in 1969.

Further down the main street in St George's Street, the ruins of the Sun Insurance office can be seen. On the opposite side of the road, the burnt out St George's Church peeps out from behind the ruins of County Hall next to it. Outside in the street, a demolition crane looms ominously.

Two of the newly arrived barrage balloons can be seen overhead, completing the wartime scene. They were rushed into Canterbury after the main bombing.

See CBB, Page 34 and BOC, Page 14 — Bottom

(Mr A. Moody: Courtesy Canterbury Museums)

You will not find the street name St George's Gate on modern street maps. It disappeared along with the crossroads in 1969, when the current round-about was built. The modern buildings in the foreground were constructed between 1957 and 1960, at which time redevelopment of the blitzed main street was complete. Only St George's tower is common to both current and old pictures.

(Paul Crampton)

This photograph was taken during the third week of June 1942 from Burgate Lane and looks along St George's Street. The cameraman is standing with St George's Gate behind him and St George's Terrace sloping away to the left. The site in the immediate foreground was once occupied by the drapers, Martins of Canterbury, at Nos. 1 to 3 St George's Street. The demolition gangs are currently at work on the next property, the west wall of which is all that is left standing. This building encompassed the premises of Francois Eldonne, the gown shop (No. 4), with the County Hall taking up the remainder (No. 3a). The large buckets of rubble were about to be loaded onto the Mount's truck for a short journey to Burgate Street and dumping into the large bomb crater there. The picture also offers a good view of the east end of St George's Church, much of which is Victorian work.

See CBB, Back Cover and BOC, Page 32 — Bottom   (Kent Messenger)

This picture, taken on 4th June 1942, is another from the prolific camera of Mr A. Moody. It shows the burnt out and partially collapsed remains of the Sun Insurance office building. It was one of a group of premises known collectively as the 'Sun Buildings'. They occupied the frontage of St George's Street near the junction with St George's Terrace and further extended along the latter as well. Curiously enough, none of the buildings were included in the numbering system for either street. Beyond the remains of the Sun Buildings can be seen further burnt out ruins in both St George's Lane and Street. All would shortly be levelled by the demolition workers.

In the foreground can be seen three discarded shovels leaning against the rubble. However, the workmen, no doubt enjoying a tea break, are nowhere to be seen!

See CBB, Page 35 — Middle
(Mr A. Moody: Courtesy Canterbury Museums)

By 1944, when this picture was taken, all blitz related demolition had been completed and the bomb sites had begun their long period of sleep. Chestnut paling fences were firmly in place and the Buddleia had begun to spread. This view was taken from practically the same spot as that featured on page 36. The 1944 photograph offers a very desolate scene. On the south side of St George's Street there is a huge void right down to Marks and Spencer in the distance. On the north side are the ruins of St George's Church, with the tower swathed in scaffolding, its fabric weakened as much by the earlier attempt to demolish it as by the fires of the Baedeker raid.

In the foreground is St George's Gate and the surviving premises of Pettit & Son at No. 1. Further along is a shed, being the first version of the temporary premises of E. & L. Bates, the gunsmiths (No. 3). In the later 1940s a larger shed would be installed.

See CBB, Page 34 and BOC, Page 14 — Bottom
(Fisk-Moore)

ST GEORGE'S TERRACE

St George's Terrace suffered terribly in the main Baedeker raid of 1st June 1942, as well as in the minor raids that followed it.

All the damaged buildings along the entire length of St George's Terrace had been demolished by July of the same year. Most of these formed a continuous terrace of elegant two- and three-storey buildings which continued from the St George's Street junction right up to the Gravel Walk slope.

The rest of the terrace was taken up by the house and grounds of 'Terrace House', a large Regency town house, occupied by Charles Dunkin — a notable veterinary practitioner. Unfortunately, Terrace House suffered the same fate as all the other houses along the city wall.

The old photograph dates from July 1942 and shows the surviving gate, perimeter fence and hedge of the former Terrace House on St George's Terrace. Beyond the perimeter wall to the right is Gravel Walk. This sloped away from St George's Terrace at right angles and reached ground level at its junction with St George's Lane.

The building visible beyond the hedge is the 1914 extension block for the Simon Langton Boys' School. This building stood on the west side of St George's Lane. Also just visible behind the perimeter wall and the evergreen tree is the St George's Lane oast house, which is featured on page 34.

The old metal gate, the fencing and the increasingly more overgrown hedge survived for many more years, probably into the 1950s. The Gravel Walk slope away from St George's Terrace was eliminated in about 1955, just prior to the construction of the new bus station. The Simon Langton School building was demolished in the summer of 1960.

(© RCHM)

The redevelopment of the 1950s was reasonably conservative and on a small scale. In the 1960s the planners and architects really let themselves go, as this current cityscape illustrates. Building was on a much larger scale and bare concrete was much more in evidence. If the aspirations of the Whitefriars Development brief are met, this entire area will be changed in the next few years.

(Paul Crampton)

This picture was taken in early July 1942 from the cattle market below St George's Terrace. It shows the three-storey late Georgian or Regency period houses at Nos. 6 to 11, just prior to their demolition. All the larger three-storey houses on the terrace (Nos. 6 to 25), were gutted by the incendiary fires of 1st June 1942. The smaller two-storey houses at the St George's Street end (Nos. 1 to 5), actually escaped damage that night. Sadly, though, they came to grief in one of the subsequent minor raids in early June and received a direct hit from a high explosive bomb. In this picture, No. 6 St George's Terrace on the far right has mostly been demolished. It is unclear if this is H.E. bomb damage, or indications that the clearance work had already started.

Many years before, local builder Walter Cozens reported that there was a Saxon arch and wall visible in one of the cellars beneath a house along St George's Terrace. Sadly, this must have been lost when the burnt out properties were pulled down.

See CBB, Page 37 — Bottom   (Fisk-Moore)

This photograph dates from the end of July 1942 and was taken at a midway point along St George's Terrace. By this time, the burnt out shells of the once elegant town houses had been demolished and little trace of them remained. The cameraman is looking down onto St George's Lane and the still standing buildings on the lane's east side. The rear of the oast house featured on pages 34 and 35 can be seen here to good advantage. The blast damage sustained by this building is evident, although it appears to be confined to the roof. The drying towers are certainly not of the conventional 'Kentish' type, found in other Canterbury oasts in nearby Dover Street or Oaten Hill. The cottages at Nos. 4 to 8 St George's Lane can be seen to the right of the oast. Further right still are the cottages at Nos. 1 to 3 that stood near to the junction with St George's Street.

(© RCHM)

The final St George's Terrace picture dates from about 1945 and looks across the cattle market pens in the foreground. The houses along the terrace have long gone. This allows for an unobstructed view of the surviving buildings in St George's Lane. On the right is the large house on the west side of the lane (No. 13) and the two remaining cottages on the east side at Nos. 7 and 8 (see also pages 34 and 35). Behind the houses can be seen the roofs and chimneys of the Simon Langton School. The telegraph pole seen in the middle distance also appears in the photograph above and provides a useful point of reference.

The city wall along this stretch looks in a very sorry state with a collapsed section and massive clumps of Red Valerian sprouting from the crumbling masonry. Red Valerian is a Mediterranean plant that has become naturalised in Britain. It likes the old walls in Canterbury and can still be found today, growing from the city wall in Broad Street.

See CBB, Page 37 — Middle (Kent Messenger)

UPPER AND LOWER BRIDGE STREET

'Early plans identified Upper and Lower Bridge Street and Broad Street as the route of the ring road, so demolition here was unmerciful.' These words were spoken by a member of the Canterbury citizens defence league, concerning the clearance of buildings with only minor blast damage.

It is true that, for whatever reason, many such buildings fronting these streets were demolished in the latter half of 1942.

In most cases, the city council were allowed to pursue the policy of demolition rather than restoration unhindered. However, in the case of at least two cherished Canterbury buildings, their demolition was halted by the personal intervention of ordinary citizens. One building was St George's Church; a story told on pages 28 to 31. The other was the Flying Horse public house in Upper Bridge Street.

This famous inn is reputed to have been built in 1574, but may have been older, at least in parts. In the 19th century a two-storey brick built extension was added at the south end, furthest from the camera.

The Flying Horse sustained blast damage in the June blitz, as can be seen in the accompanying old photograph, taken on the 18th of that month. An early decision must have been made to pull down the inn, as it has been reported that materials were removed from the Flying Horse, to repair damaged buildings elsewhere.

In any case, one day in the late summer of 1942, local architect Anthony Swaine was walking past the Flying Horse when he noticed men on the roof who were throwing tiles down onto the road below. He asked what they were doing, and one replied 'we are demolishing it mate!' At that very moment, Tony noticed his friend, Mr Tomlinson — a senior assessor to the War Damage Commission — coming down the road and together they intervened. Mr Tomlinson used his authority and demolition was stopped forthwith.

(© RCHM)

Thankfully, the Flying Horse was subsequently restored and is greatly appreciated by both citizens and tourists alike. In Upper Bridge Street today, the Flying Horse is the only pre-war building to be found. There would be none at all, if the demolition workers had been allowed to finish their work. A good position to view this inn is from the city wall ramparts opposite.

(Paul Crampton)

This scene of destruction could be found on the same side of Upper Bridge Street as the Flying Horse, but north of the junction with Dover Street. Six properties at Nos. 4 to 9 Upper Bridge Street were destroyed along this stretch. This particular photograph shows the burnt out and collapsed premises of the Canterbury and District Co-operative Society butchers at No. 8. The huge three-storey party wall with the two chimney stacks divided Nos. 8 and 9. The latter shop was W. Peters, the baker, and it stood on the corner with Dover Street. The other ruins seen on the left of the picture belong to destroyed buildings in Dover Street.

Apart from the Co-op butchers, other businesses to lose their premises included F.R. Biggleston, ironmongers. In the 1950s both of these businesses rebuilt new premises on the sites of their former buildings.
See BOC, Page 30 — Bottom   (Mr A. Moody)

Much of the damage sustained in the June 1942 raids was as a result of incendiary bomb fires. Not so the devastation seen here in Lower Bridge Street, which was caused by a high explosive bomb. The collapsed building in the foreground was once the premises of Tice & Co., ironmongers, at No. 6 Lower Bridge Street. The damaged but still standing building beyond is the premises of J. Hoare, fruiterer and greengrocer (No. 5).

During clearing up operations it was decided that much of Mr Hoare's building was beyond repair and the upper two storeys were dismantled. However, the ground floor section was retained and continued to trade as a fruit and vegetable shop until 1968. Tice & Co. later erected a single-storey building on the site of their collapsed premises. Both of these single-storey shops were finally pulled down in 1969, when Lower Bridge Street became a dual carriageway.
See TAN, Page 21 — Bottom   (Mr A. Moody)

The rubble and rafters strewn across the foreground in this view are all that is left of the premises of Dashwood toy dealer at Nos. 8 to 10 Lower Bridge Street. Sadly, the high explosive bomb attack here caused loss of life.

The buildings beyond the blitzed site are situated on either side of Burgate Lane. Nearest the camera and next to Zoar Chapel are the premises of J.C. Elvy & Co., builders and decorators. This building soon had its roof removed and had been almost completely demolished by the end of the 1940s. Most fascinating of all are the cottages on the west side of Burgate Lane. These are built largely of Caen stone, recovered from the redundant and ruinous abbey church of St Augustine, in the years following the dissolution. The terrace of cottages was demolished in the 1950s, just prior to the redevelopment of the area.
See BOC, Page 16 — Top and TAN, Page 21 — Bottom   (Mr A. Moody)

In 1969, when the road became a dual carriageway, it was the north side that was used. Consequently, some of the original late Georgian and Regency buildings can still be found on the south side of St George's Place. Today the Martin Walter premises are empty and have an uncertain future. Demolition and the redevelopment of the whole site will be the probable outcome.

(Paul Crampton)

ST GEORGE'S PLACE

Much of St George's Place was destroyed by intense incendiary fires in the small hours of 1st June 1942. Most of the north side was burnt to the ground. There were a number of photographs taken at the time, some of which can be seen on page 43.

The south side fared better in the June blitz. Consequently, pictures of the damage it did suffer are quite rare. This view shows all that was left of No. 39 St George's Place, on the south side, after it had been ravaged by fire. The 1940 Kelly's Street Directory shows this building as the premises of Keating and Miskin Ltd: refrigeration engineer. It also contained the flats for three private residents in the upper storeys. The water heater from one of the destroyed flats can be seen still clinging to the surviving rear wall of the property. Next door at No. 40, the tobacconist and post office run by Mrs Bessie Powell was similarly destroyed.

On the left of the photograph is the edge of the Baptist Church, which survived the blitz. It can still be found in St George's Place today. The church was built in 1860, largely behind the existing buildings that stood on the street frontage. Therefore, for a while the church was rather hemmed in. However, this problem was solved in the early years of this century by the demolition of the property at No. 38 St George's Place, which once adjoined the destroyed house in the old picture.

In the mid to late 1940s the only evidence of the destroyed buildings was fenced off open cellars containing Buddleia. During this time, behind the cellars and on a former garden area, Martin Walter Ltd constructed several large temporary sheds.

In the early 1950s these were replaced by a permanent garage building that covered the whole site.

(Mr A. Moody)

The north side of St George's Place was one mass of flames following the incendiary attack on the night of 1st June 1942. Only a few properties nearest St George's crossroads escaped the fire. A contemporary account from a resident speaks of little or no fire watching prior to the conflagration and then, little or no fire fighting once the flames had taken hold. Fire fighting resources in the city that night were stretched to the limit. St George's Place was one thoroughfare too many and no serious fire fighting took place until everything was well alight and collapsing. The following morning little could be found of the long row of brick built late Georgian town houses, save for a few chimney stacks and party walls.

This photograph was taken a few days later and before the demolition crews had started work. The cleared passage in the foreground leads to the premises of builder Browning, Deanne & Co. Ltd, parts of which escaped destruction.

See CBB, Page 46 and BOC, Page 16 — Bottom
(Mr A. Moody: Courtesy Canterbury Museums)

Nearby Lower Chantry Lane also suffered considerable damage in the June blitz. A row of ancient cottages near the junction with St George's Place, at Nos. 4 to 9 Lower Chantry Lane, were destroyed that night. Next to these cottages was a large three-storey detached house, known as 'Chantry House', that was situated in large grounds. The roof of Chantry House had suffered some incendiary fire damage, but the rest of the structure was sound. It therefore made little sense to demolish the property, a process carried out in July 1942. The Ministry of Works picture shows this demolition work in progress. As can be seen from the mutilated remains, there is no evidence of fire damage.

The front entrance to Chantry House had Roman Doric style columns at either side of it. One of these collapsed columns can be seen in the centre of the photograph.

See CBB, Page 49 — Top Left   (© RCHM)

Returning to St George's Place, this picture was taken in about August of 1942. By this time many of the ruined houses had been flattened, although a sizeable portion of No. 16, the premises of Robert Brett & Sons Ltd, was still standing. These particular remains can also be seen in the top picture, in the foreground. The demolition and clearance has opened up a view of Bell Harry tower, above which a barrage balloon can be seen hovering. The buildings that stood on this corner dated from the late 18th and early 19th century period. The vast majority of these were built as prestigious houses, but by the 1930s many had been taken over by insurance companies.

After the blitz of Canterbury, this corner site remained empty for many years. Much of it was eventually swallowed up for road widening, first for Lower Chantry Lane in 1956 and finally for St George's Place in 1969.

See CBB, Page 47 — Top, BOC, Page 17 — Top and TAN, Page 36   (Kent Messenger)

43

LADY WOOTTON'S GREEN — NORTH SIDE

The survival of buildings from former monastic orders after the dissolution of 1538 to 1540 depended on their being found a new use. In Canterbury, sections of the Whitefriars, Greyfriars, Blackfriars, St Gregory's and St Sepulchre's were converted for residential use.

In the case of St Augustine's Abbey, their large cathedral-like church was mostly demolished, but the other ex-monastic buildings were converted into a royal palace for King Henry VIII and succeeding monarchs.

The then and now photographs show another building once associated with St Augustine's Abbey, which has also survived because it was adapted to a new use. In the days before the dissolution it was the Almonry Chapel which, according to William Somner, dated from 1237. The Almonry was part of a monastery where alms were distributed to the poor. In some places, as here, it was situated outside the walls of the order, so the lay folk did not interfere with the running of the order.

The building survived the dissolution of the monastery. However, by 1640 when William Somner wrote his 'Antiquities of Canterbury', it was 'desolate and rotting in its own ruins'. By the mid 1700s a large and impressive Georgian house had been built onto the remains of the chapel.

Had this not happened, then it is unlikely that any trace of the former chapel would be surviving today. Some of the medieval work is now plastered over (see opposite), but there are still visible areas of flint work preserved within the walls of this attractive house.

See BOC, Page 47 — Bottom (© RCHM)

It is fortunate that this fine Georgian house was retained after the blitz, when all the other buildings in Lady Wootton's Green were demolished. The best visible traces of medieval fabric can be found in and against the west wall (left side) of the house and also in parts of the rear elevation. Other traces of the Almonry Chapel can be seen in the west wall of the cellar.

(Paul Crampton)

Approximately one third of the north side of Lady Wootton's Green was taken up by a large 'L'-shaped house that stood on the corner with Broad Street and was actually numbered in the latter street's sequence. This house, known as 'The Priory', employed amounts of re-used ecclesiastical masonry in its construction, probably recovered from the demolished St Augustine's Abbey Church. The ground floor walls were constructed in a chequer pattern of alternate Caen stone blocks and red brick. A remaining portion of this elaborate wall can be seen on the left of the picture, taken by the Ministry of Works in July 1942. The Priory had sustained minor fire damage in the June blitz but, according to war damage assessor Anthony Swaine, was capable of repair. Nevertheless, and not surprisingly, it was demolished. Tony Swaine managed to recover a wooden gargoyle from the demolition workers' bonfire of ancient timbers. It is now in the Heritage Museum.

See CBB, Page 55 — Top Right   (© RCHM)

The Georgian town house at No. 1 Lady Wootton's Green was badly blasted in the Baedeker raid, as the picture opposite amply testifies. The photograph seen on this page was taken in the late summer of 1942, by which time some restoration work had already been carried out. This involved re-tiling most of the roof and rebuilding the chimney stack nearest the camera. On the left of the picture is the garden of the now demolished house, 'The Priory'. Behind can be seen an ancient flint wall, probably part of the old monastic Almonry.

During later renovation work on this surviving house, the ivy and old plaster were stripped from the front elevation. This revealed a substantial flint wall with stone dressing. Set in the wall were stone jambs in a gothic pattern, relating to a window or door of the former chapel. Sadly, the wall was hacked back, re-rendered and the remains once more hidden.

(© RCHM)

Up until 1942 there was another surviving building from the former St Augustine's Abbey Almonry in Lady Wootton's Green. This was the Almonry Hall, a long and fairly low building next to the former chapel but at right angles to the street. After the dissolution the Almonry Hall became a school, then the meeting place for the Canterbury Congregational Church from about 1660 onwards. It was subsequently divided up into cottages and the hall's continued existence was guaranteed for many more years.

The associated picture shows the house at No. 2 Lady Wootton's Green. This probably represented the southern end of the hall, with the rest stretching away behind. Other adjacent cottages on the street frontage, and at right angles to the main hall, were flattened in the June blitz. Later plaster work, now blasted away, hid the true antiquity of this surviving building.

All of the Almonry Hall survived the June blitz (see also page 32), albeit in a blasted state. Sadly, though, it was subsequently demolished, probably in early 1943.

See CBB, Page 52   (© RCHM)

LADY WOOTTON'S GREEN — SOUTH SIDE

In the blitz of Canterbury more damage was caused to the north-east quadrant of the city by high explosive bombs than by incendiary bombs. Lady Wootton's Green took a particular hammering during the Baedeker raid and many of its ancient buildings came to grief. However, rather than receiving direct hits, most of the old buildings here suffered varying degrees of blast damage.

Such was the case with this ancient 15th century house situated on the corner of Lady Wootton's Green and Monastery Street. The photograph was taken during the first week of June 1942. All of the lath and plaster in-fill on the upper storey had been blasted away, as have the roof tiles and chimney stack. A few of the supporting timbers had also been dislodged, but in spite of this, the ancient timber frame had stood up pretty well to the high explosive onslaught.

This house is typical of many constructed in the south-east of England after 1400. The usual building material was locally grown oak. As originally constructed, many of these houses had a central hall with no first floor level above it and an opening in the roof to let out the smoke from a centrally placed hearth. They were later 'modernised' by the insertion of brick chimney stacks and the provision of a first floor level over the central bays to provide more bedrooms.

In the late 1930s this building, at No. 4a Lady Wootton's Green, was the residence and business premises of haulage contractor Ambrose Rose. The building had clearly been adapted to this purpose some years before.

The house seen further along Lady Wootton's Green is the one survivor of a pair of 17th century semi-detached houses. It had sustained severe damage and may have been beyond repair.

See CBB, Page 53 — Middle

(© RCHM)

The planners of the new Lady Wootton's Green shunned modernism. These houses were built in the 1950s along very traditional lines. In fact, pro-modernist planners at the time were horrified by the use of 'Georgian' door cases. Today Lady Wootton's Green is an attractive area, spoilt only by its current use as a traffic rat run.

(Paul Crampton)

This photograph was taken in the first week of June 1942, at about the same time as the picture on the opposite page. It shows the heavy damage sustained by a pair of 17th century timber framed semi-detached houses, at Nos. 5 and 6 Lady Wootton's Green. The house nearest the camera has been blasted completely flat, whilst the remaining one, although still standing, has sustained serious damage. None of the timbers, either standing or fallen, show any sign of fire damage.

As mentioned opposite, unlike the 15th century timber framed house, this 17th century one was probably beyond reasonable repair. A Ministry of Works picture taken in July (not reproduced here) shows the house having been pulled down, but left as a pile of fallen timbers. An observer seeing the house for the first time at this later date might assume that the demolition was caused by enemy action.
See CBB, Page 53 — Bottom
(Mr A. Moody: Courtesy Canterbury Museums)

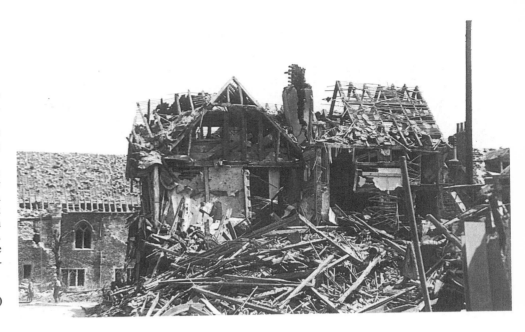

By the time the 15th century house was first photographed in early June 1942 (as seen on page 46) its fate had probably already been decided. It was to go. Initially, though, the survival of much of the sturdy oak frame made it difficult to justify complete demolition. During the next few weeks the supporting upper storey timbers were pulled away, presumably by demolition workers, and the roof was allowed to collapse.

When the Ministry of Works came to examine and photograph the damaged ancient buildings of Canterbury in July 1942, much demolition work had already been carried out. Their photograph of the 15th century house is reproduced here. As can be seen, they found only the ground floor portion of the building intact, with a pile of collapsed timbers above it. There was now little worth saving and eventually these remains were also pulled down.
See CBB, Page 53 — Middle   (© RCHM)

The city wall along Broad Street provides a good vantage point from which to photograph Lady Wootton's Green. This picture was taken at the end of 1942 and shows both sides of the Green, as well as St Augustine's Abbey at the far end. On the north side (left of the picture) are the two buildings once associated with the Almonry, as described on pages 44 and 45. On the right hand side of Lady Wootton's Green can be seen the empty site once occupied by the 15th and 17th century timber framed houses, as seen in the pictures above and opposite. During clearing up operations in the autumn of 1942 a massive bonfire was made of all the ancient demolished timbers from both houses. Many hundreds of years of Canterbury history went up in smoke.

Repair work has already started on the badly blasted abbey buildings. At this stage, priority was given to the roofs and any portion of the building in danger of collapse.
See BOC, Page 7 — Top Right   (Fisk-Moore)

(Above) A close up view of the eastern end of Burgate Street showing the many surviving buildings. The lofty facade of Starrs House is still standing. The house on the opposite side of the street shows some incendiary fire damage to the roof. Other buildings show only minor blast damage with many missing roof tiles. Beyond Burgate Street can be seen Burgate Lane and the buildings which survived until the 1960s.

(Mr A. Moody)

(Below) A study of the devastation in Iron Bar Lane and along the middle section of Burgate Street (south side). The large depository building in Iron Bar Lane stands open to the elements. Nothing remains of the beautiful timbered houses once to be found in Burgate Street. Still surviving is St Mary Magdalene tower and St Thomas' Catholic Church beyond, both with only minor damage.

(Mr A. Moody)

(Above) A superb study of the area around the four-ton bomb crater, to be found on the north side of Burgate Street. It is mid June 1942 and the crater is covered in camouflage netting. In the foreground is the surviving half of Canon Crum's house in the south precincts. The collapsed remains of the other half can be seen to the left. The lush foliage of the trees in the precincts is very impressive.

(Mr A. Moody)

(Below) The same area in August 1942. By this time the camouflage netting was off and the crater rapidly filling with brick rubble brought in by the lorry load from the clearance operations. In the foreground, the remains of Canon Crum's house are being demolished. Beyond the crater, the remains of cottages in Iron Bar Lane have gone, although the damaged depository building is still standing.

(Fisk-Moore)

The house here today on the corner of Broad Street with Lady Wootton's Green is part of the same development seen in the current picture on page 46. At the time this house was put up, it was imagined that Broad Street would soon become part of the city ring road, by eliminating the car park opposite. This never came to pass and, consequently, many buildings were saved, especially those in Lower Broad Street.

(Paul Crampton)

BROAD STREET

The top half of Broad Street sustained much bomb damage in the blitz of Canterbury and this was mostly of the high explosive sort. Along the east side of the street between the Church Street St Paul's junction and the Brewer's Delight public house, there were 32 properties of varying sizes and functions. The bombing accounted for half of these buildings.

Notable amongst the destroyed buildings of Broad Street were the Comet Inn (Nos. 4 and 5), Hardres Dairy (No. 10b) and the delightful house near the Lady Wootton's Green junction known as The Priory (No. 21).

The survivors were as follows: Boorman & Sons butchers at No. 1 Broad Street. Next were a pair of cottages (Nos. 2 and 3) and after a gap, three more houses (Nos. 8, 9 and 10), all of which were undamaged. Then, after another gap, came the properties at Nos. 16 to 18a Broad Street, some of which can be seen in the accompanying old photograph.

Number 16 is to the right of the picture, with a tarpaulin covering the roof. This is the cottage of Mr John Anderson. To the left of this, with loosened lath and plaster, is the antique shop of Mr R. Todd at No. 17. Both of these buildings are timber framed and probably date from the 16th century. Just visible on the left of the photograph are the brick built premises of electrical engineer Sydney Orton.

The remaining survivors were a row of cottages beyond Lady Wootton's Green at Nos. 22 to 26 Broad Street, also with moderate blast damage.

Eventually, only the undamaged cottages below No. 10 were retained. The others, including those pictured here, were demolished.

See CBB, Page 55 — Bottom

(Kent Messenger)

This panoramic view was taken in the middle of June 1942 and shows buildings in Broad Street, Lady Wootton's Green and Monastery Street. It is interesting to compare this with the later picture reproduced on page 47, and taken after clearing up operations. The white-painted brick building in the foreground is the premises of Sydney Orton, electrical engineers, at No. 18 Broad Street. (It can also be seen on the left hand side of the picture on page 50.) Earlier this century the building at No. 18 was a pub known as The Three Cups. Right on the corner with Lady Wootton's Green is the single-storey sweet shop run by Mr Wilson (No. 18a).

The Orton premises, together with the adjacent timber framed buildings seen on page 50, had all sustained blast damage, but were capable of repair and retention. They were demolished, probably in the winter of 1942 through to 1943.
See CBB, Page 55 — Bottom   (© RCHM)

This is a picture of the partially demolished house, known as The Priory, that stood on the northern corner of Broad Street with Lady Wootton's Green. A view of these remains from the Lady Wootton's Green frontage can be seen on page 45. The window in the wall still standing to the left was rescued by Anthony Swaine and later installed in a medieval house in Sturry. Today Diocesan House stands on this corner site.
See CBB, Page 54   (© RCHM)

These are the surviving houses at Nos. 22 to 26 Broad Street. New glass has been installed and work is currently in hand to secure the roofs. It is obviously the intention to retain these houses. Sadly, though, they received further damage in the daylight raid of October 1942 and were later demolished. The two houses on the right are brick built and of 19th century origin. The three on the left are timber framed, at least above the jetty, and are probably 17th century.
See CBB, Page 54   (Kent Messenger)

Right at the top end of Broad Street could be found the premises of William Boorman, the family butcher. They stood on the junction with Church Street St Paul's, where the tank traps can be seen. This photograph has appeared a number of times in print before as it perfectly captures the 'business as usual' spirit of wartime Canterbury. High explosive bomb damage has destroyed the upper living quarters but has spared the shop, which was able to continue to trade after some essential repair work. War damage assessor Anthony Swaine well remembers surveying this property before it re-opened. He was taking down some details in the cellar when he turned round and got the fright of his life. He found himself virtually nose to nose with a bull's head on a shelf that was crawling with maggots.

To the left of the picture can be seen the surviving house at No. 2 Broad Street; one of a pair that survived well into the 1950s.
See BOC, Page 34 — Bottom   (Kent Messenger)

Many buildings at the east end of Burgate Street survived the blitz and can still be seen today. The new shop built on the site of Starrs House (see opposite) in the early 1950s followed a very traditional pattern, in marked contrast to new shops then going up in St George's Street. St Mary Magdalene tower, a lucky survivor of the blitz, continues to grace this section of Burgate Street.

(Paul Crampton)

BURGATE STREET — EAST END

This attractive tower standing on the south side of Burgate Street once formed part of the parish church of St Mary Magdalene. The church was not destroyed in the blitz as some people think, but had been demolished many years before.

The St Mary Magdalene parish had united with that of St George's in 1681. The church closed in 1866 and much of it was pulled down five years later. Most of the demolished material was re-used in the construction of the new north aisle for St George's Church in 1872.

St Mary Magdalene tower dates from 1503 and was built onto the existing church, which was then about 300 years old. This former church tower is unique in Canterbury in that it is largely constructed from stone blocks. The more usual building material of flint can be found in the lower portions of the east side (nearest the camera), as well as on the south and west sides of the tower. This is probably where the 'new' tower was bonded onto the existing body of the church, which was of flint construction. Some of this flint fabric may therefore date from about 1200.

The old photograph dates from June 1943 and shows the tower still wearing its battle scars. It did indeed have a lucky escape in the blitz, being only yards from the edge of the four-ton bomb crater on the opposite side of the street. A temporary wall can be seen across the gothic arch of the tower. This was built to protect the monuments contained therein from blast damage.

Further along on the south side of Burgate Street can be seen a huge void left by the bombing of the previous year. Where once stood a venerable treasury of timber framed houses, there is now only a chestnut paling fence.

See BOC, Page 9 — Top Right

(© RCHM)

Another view of St Mary Magdalene tower, this time from the west side. It is dated 31st May 1943. The scar of the demolished building that once adjoined the west face of the tower can clearly be seen. This lost three-storey timber framed house was built after the tower and had no east wall of its own. To the right of the tower is surviving masonry from the west end of the body of the church. This portion was not demolished along with the rest of the church in 1872, as it also adjoined the lost house.

Beyond the tower can be seen the Roman Catholic church of St Thomas, built in 1874. It suffered minor blast damage in the blitz the year before, but otherwise escaped unscathed. St Thomas' Church was designed by Canterbury architect John Green Hall, who was also responsible for the Congregational Church in Guildhall Street, now part of Debenhams.

See CBB, Page 59 — Left and BOC, Page 44 — Top Left   (© RCHM)

This spectacular ruin is all that is left of a substantial three-storey Georgian building, known as Starrs House, following the June 1942 blitz. Starrs House stood against the north side of Burgate Street but with its back to that thoroughfare. It actually faced inwards towards the south precincts of the Cathedral and came under the auspices of the Dean and Chapter. The standing wall here, therefore, represents the front of the house, as seen from the rear garden of No. 11 Burgate Street. The 1874 Ordnance Survey map of Canterbury shows Starrs House walled off from Burgate Street. However, by the 1930s the wall was gone and shop premises had been constructed into the ground floor rear section of the building to face the street. This was occupied by the National Cash Register Co. Ltd, as No. 10 Burgate Street. The rest of the house was still in residential use by the Dean and Chapter, as No. 14D The Precincts.

See BOC, Page 13 — Top and Page 34 — Middle   (© RCHM)

This view was taken in July 1942 by the Ministry of Works, who were responsible for all the pictures on this page and the one opposite. The cameraman is standing in an area of the south precincts known as 'The Oaks', and looks south towards the eastern end of Burgate Street. The lofty and still ivy-clad facade of Starrs House once more dominates the scene. Through its ruined windows can be seen some surviving buildings on the south side of Burgate Street. Dead centre is the three-storey building containing the City of Canterbury District Nursing Association Institute (No. 62). To the left, in lighter coloured rendering, is No. 63 Burgate Street, which housed a number of associations as diverse as the Canterbury & District Grocers' Association and the Church of England Temperance Society and Mission to Hop-pickers!

On the right of the picture is the rear elevation of the house and shop at Nos. 11 and 12 Burgate Street (north side). This, latterly, housed the Misses E. & L. Barrow and their sweet shop.

(© RCHM)

BURGATE STREET — NORTH SIDE (CENTRAL)

The city of Canterbury was the last target in the brief series of Baedeker raids, which concentrated on the historical cities and towns of England.

The Luftwaffe's aim was to flatten the ancient centres of these places and, thereby, destroy the morale of their citizens. On both counts they failed. Although large sections of each target city were destroyed, the Cathedrals of Exeter, Norwich and Canterbury as well as the Minster at York escaped with only minor scars.

Some have said that the Luftwaffe were not really trying to destroy the cathedrals. In Canterbury, at least, this was not the case. As well as the high explosive bombs and thousands of incendiaries, a single 4-ton bomb was brought over and its target was to be the Cathedral. Whilst the Baedeker raid was being pressed home, the plane carrying the special bomb dived at the Cathedral. Fortunately, the pilot missed, but it was a near miss!

The resultant explosion blew open a massive crater some 20 feet deep and about 40 yards in diameter. The edge of the crater fell only 50 yards short of the south-west transept of the Cathedral. The crater, covered in camouflage netting, can be seen in the old photograph, taken from Burgate Street.

The near miss may have saved the Cathedral, but the 4-ton bomb explosion destroyed several buildings in the south precincts, as well as a large section of Burgate Street. As soon as the June raids had subsided, the camouflage netting was removed and it was discovered that the crater had filled with water. This new inner city lake soon attracted the attention of skimming swallows. But, alas, this ornithological treat was short lived.

The crater was gradually filled with tons of brick rubble brought by the lorry load from the nearby blitzed streets.

See BOC, Page 46 — Middle

(Mr A. Moody: Courtesy Canterbury Museums)

This new arcade of shops appeared in 1950: the first retail premises to be built on a bomb site in Canterbury. They were partly financed by the Canadian government. At the same time, new houses in the south precincts behind were being developed by the Dean and Chapter. The dummy chimneys above these shops provided much amusement for the more modernist architects at the time.

(Paul Crampton)

Another view of the bomb crater, as seen from Burgate Street on 4th June 1942. The depth of the crater has been painted onto a steel joist, which was all that was left of one of the buildings destroyed by the 4-ton bomb. In fact, the steel joist that once supported the weight of the upper storeys above the shop front has now been half buried by the earth displaced from the huge crater behind.

Dean Hewlett Johnson, mug of tea in hand, can be seen scrambling up the earth mound to where the camouflage netting stretches across the void. No doubt, he is acquiring some last minute details of the spectacle from the soldier with him. This information can then be imparted to the Duke of Kent, when he visits this site later the same day.

The western towers and nave of the Cathedral make an impressive backdrop to this scene of destruction.

See BOC, Page 23 — Middle and Bottom
(Mr A. Moody: Courtesy Canterbury Museums)

Burgate Street was not the only victim of the 4-ton bomb. A large house in the Cathedral precincts was also blown in half. The house in question was the residence of Canon Crum at No. 13 The Precincts. The eastern half of the house was literally flattened, whilst the other half escaped with blast damage. This picture, taken in July 1942 from the north (with the Cathedral behind the photographer) shows the remaining half of the house being pulled down. Note the exposed radiators in the half-demolished upstairs rooms. A view of the house from the south can be seen in the picture above. Other views of Canon Crum's house, both before and during demolition, can be seen in the cityscape photographs on page 49.

Today the area is occupied by the houses in South Close, a post-war development of dwellings by the Dean and Chapter.

(© RCHM)

By the end of July 1942, when this picture was taken, the crater was already half-filled with many tons of bricks and mortar, brought in from the bomb sites all around. Many thousands of Tudor bricks and pieces of moulded plasterwork must have been dumped into this convenient hole in the ground during those weeks of demolition and clearance. This photograph was probably taken from the upper story of the halved residence of Canon Crum, during its demolition. To the right of the picture is the St Mary Magdalene tower and St Thomas' Catholic Church (see page 53). On the left is the lucky survivor at No. 15 Burgate Street. This late medieval building originally had a side garden and no adjoining properties to the west, as the 1874 Ordnance Survey map makes clear. The collapsed building seen here on the edge of the crater must therefore be a fairly recent 'in-fill' construction. They are not timbers, but steel girders embedded in the exposed brick party wall.

(© RCHM)

BURGATE STREET — SOUTH SIDE (CENTRAL)

In the last 50 years there have been many changes to the five lanes that branch off from the south side of Burgate Street. Before 1942 they were all very narrow and each contained a wealth of old buildings of both timber and brick construction. However, each lane had its own individual character.

Burgate Lane was crowded with a miscellany of terraced houses, with a small non-conformist chapel hidden amongst them. Canterbury Lane was a real mixture, containing, amongst other things, a primary school and a 1920s bakery building. Iron Bar Lane went to both extremes with its tiny cottages as well as two large furniture depositories.

Butchery Lane was more retail in nature and contained three public houses. Mercery Lane was the grandest and most famous of all the lanes, with its prestigious shops and buildings.

The blitz affected most of the lanes and some more than others. The outside lanes in the sequence were least affected. For example, Burgate Lane was damaged only at one end and Mercery Lane escaped completely unscathed.

The central lane in the series, Iron Bar Lane, was worst affected, as can be seen in the accompanying photograph, taken from Burgate Street early in June 1942. Following the Baedeker raid, all that was left standing in this lane was the blitzed shell of a depository building that was soon demolished. There were also two small brick garages which survived for another ten years.

The pile of charred timbers and sheets of corrugated iron in the foreground is all that is left of the old Crown Inn that once stood on the corner of Iron Bar Lane with Burgate Street. The corrugated iron came from a temporary roof that was constructed over the inn, following damage sustained in a minor raid some 18 months previously.

See CBB, Page 59 — Left   (Kent Messenger)

The utilitarian shops built along the south side of Burgate Street between 1957 and 1960 were not so impressive as those put up in St George's Street in the early 1950s. This pointed the way towards a decline in aesthetic standards of architecture in the 1960s, exemplified by the shoe box Longmarket development. Iron Bar Lane contains some very plain single-storey shops, one of which is visible on the left.

(Paul Crampton)

The south side of Burgate Street between Iron Bar Lane and Butchery Lane was particularly rich in fine timber framed buildings from the 16th and 17th centuries. One especially fine example was the double-jettied building at No. 54, more famously known as The Burgate Farmhouse Tea Rooms, run by the Misses Hawkins. Like many timber framed buildings in the centre of Canterbury, it had been extended at the rear during the nineteenth and early twentieth centuries. These hidden extensions were usually of brick construction. Sadly, also like many timbered buildings in this part of the city, it fell victim to the incendiary attack of 1st June 1942, and was then flattened by the blast from the huge bomb that fell opposite.

This picture was taken from inside the ruins of the old Farmhouse Tea Rooms and looks towards what is left of the later brick rear extension.

See BOC, Page 9 — Left   (Mr A. Moody)

Another general view of the flattened south side of Burgate Street, taken slightly earlier than the picture on page 56, judging by the extent of the demolition and clearance. The ruins of the Crown Inn can clearly be seen to the left of the picture. In the centre of the photograph, clearance workers enjoy the hospitality of the Catholic Women's League of Friends' mobile canteen. The arduous clearing up operations were carried out by local workmen and members of the armed forces. They were augmented by Italian prisoners of war. One local lady whose house was blitzed told me that some of the POWs were wont to loot the demolished dwellings for any valuables they could find! One would hope that this practice was not widespread.

(Mr A. Moody: Courtesy Canterbury Museums)

Further along Burgate Street, and nearer the rear gateway to the Longmarket, could once be found the extensive premises of Court Bros (Furnishers) Ltd. The accompanying picture shows the completely flattened site that was once part of their premises, at No. 50 Burgate Street. It consisted of a charming narrow double-jettied timber building with two gables, and a brick building that was adjacent to the aforementioned gateway. On the left of the photograph are the twisted girders of Edward Moss, the ladies' hairdressing salon. This building (No. 51) gave the appearance of being of recent construction.

The low building running across the picture, with the iron clerestory roof, is the covered passageway leading into the Corn Exchange and Longmarket building. Beyond the Longmarket gateway in Burgate Street were further premises belonging to Courts.

See BOC, Page 9 — Bottom Right and Page 13 — Middle   (Mr A. Moody)

BURGATE STREET — WEST END

Thankfully, the western end of Burgate Street was spared in the bombing. How very much worse the loss to our heritage could have been had the incendiary fires spread along to the Buttermarket!

Fortunately, and largely due to skilled fire fighting, the flames were halted just short of Butchery Lane on the south side of Burgate Street. On the north side the 4-ton bomb aimed at the Cathedral instead took out a large middle section of the street's buildings. Ironically, this may have helped to stop the spread of fire westwards on this side of Burgate Street.

The accompanying old photograph was taken on 4th June 1942, by Mr A. Moody, during the visit by the Duke of Kent. The Duke, who was the younger brother of King George VI, toured the main areas of devastation in Canterbury. He can be seen here with the touring party, inspecting the edge of the 4-ton bomb crater. A part of the camouflage netting spread over the crater can be seen at the bottom of the picture.

The Royal touring party in the picture includes the Mayor, Charles Lefevre, Dean Hewlett Johnson and the Chief Constable, George Hall. Veteran Canterbury photographer, Mr W. Fisk-Moore, can also be seen second from the left. He took many pictures of the Duke's visit to the city, all of which can be seen in the book 'The Blitz Of Canterbury'.

In the background, the buildings on either side of Burgate Street mark the limit of the destruction. On the south (left) side can be seen the surviving Longmarket rear gateway, then, after a gap, the premises of Penn & Co., house furnishers.

On the north side, the blasted premises of Charles Cheshire — bookseller — were demolished within days of this picture being taken.

See CBB, Page 57 — Bottom and TAN, Page 8 (Mr A. Moody)

The current picture looks through the arches of the 1950 shop arcade towards the brand new Longmarket development. Both sets of building borrow heavily from the styles of the past, resulting in the use of dummy chimney stacks and other 'features' to fool the passer-by. Most people like the new Longmarket. All I can say is that it is better than the bland 1960s complex it replaced.

(Paul Crampton)

As mentioned on page 57, there were further premises of Courts Brothers on the western side of the Longmarket rear gateway. This other shop at No. 47/49 Burgate Street was burnt to the ground as the accompanying picture amply illustrates. The word 'Courts' can just be made out on the scorched remains of the shop frontage. Yet another Courts shop was situated on the north side of Burgate Street and opposite the destroyed shops. This third shop survived the blitz.

The building seen on the right of the photograph was the premises of a rival firm of house furnishers, namely Penn & Co. This damaged structure was patched up and later taken over by Courts. Unfortunately, in January 1955 this shop caught fire and had to be partially demolished. All trace of it was finally removed in 1959, just prior to the redevelopment of the Longmarket site.

(Mr A. Moody)

Having examined the large crater on the north side of the street, the Duke of Kent and the royal party moved towards the Buttermarket. The Duke is seen here en route, talking to Mr H. Snashall, a member of the National Fire Service. He asked the fireman if there had been many fires and received the reply, 'just a few!' This gross understatement of the situation on 1st June has obviously amused the Mayor, Alderman Charles Lefevre, who is looking on from the left of the picture.

Behind the fireman are the surviving buildings at the west end of Burgate Street that he and his colleagues helped to save on the dreadful night of the Baedeker raid. The Victorian buildings in the background date from 1865 and were built to fill the gap in Sun Street, after the disastrous fire of the same year.

(Mr A. Moody: Courtesy Canterbury Museums)

As well as by the photographers Mr A. Moody and Mr W. Fisk-Moore, the royal party were followed round by journalists from the Kent Messenger and Kentish Gazette. The Gazette representative managed to record some conversations between the Duke and various citizens of Canterbury as he went on his tour. This picture was taken at the Buttermarket with Christ Church Gate on the right and Sun Street on the left. The people of Canterbury, both young and old, all have their eyes fixed on the Duke as he talks to Mrs C.M. Evans. Mr and Mrs Evans ran a nearby newsagents shop in Burgate Street that had survived the blitz intact.

After talking to a few other people in the Buttermarket, the Duke passed through the Christ Church Gate and toured the ravaged Cathedral precincts, in the company of the Dean.

(Mr A. Moody)

THE CATHEDRAL AND THE SOUTH PRECINCTS

During the Baedeker raid on Canterbury, a number of high explosive bombs fell onto the northern precincts of the Cathedral. One destroyed the west end of the King's School dining hall, formerly the Christ Church Priory Brew House. Another blew the top off the Forrens Gate and left a crater in the Green Court. A third HE bomb destroyed the Cathedral library.

The accompanying photograph was taken in July 1942, during clearing up operations, and shows the extent of the damage to the fabric of the library. In the foreground, materials salvaged from the wreckage have been neatly piled for possible re-use.

The explosion also caused damage to the adjacent Chapter House, where a fracture was discovered in the north wall running from floor to ceiling. Furthermore, the nearby Wibert water tower and the Dark Entry sustained blast damage.

The Cathedral library was not as old as its ruins would suggest. It was built in 1868, on a site once occupied by the south end of the Great Dorter. This was the monastic dormitory built in 1080 by Archbishop Lanfranc. The Victorian library had incorporated some ancient fragments of the dorter, but luckily, most of these escaped destruction.

More substantial remains of the Great Dorter can be seen at its north end, adjacent to the Larder Gate. The north end survived the post dissolution demolition of the 1540s to which much of the dorter succumbed, as it was converted into houses for the newly-established Dean and Chapter.

See BOC, Page 39 — Right and Page 47 — Top Right   (Fisk-Moore)

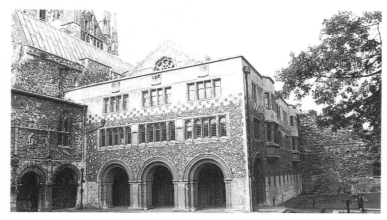

The new replacement library was constructed on the same site and opened in July 1954. The designer was John Denman who managed to produce an appropriate looking building on such a sensitive site. The later red bricked Wolfson library of 1966, above the Dark Entry, is also a success.

(Paul Crampton)

This second, much closer, view of the ruined library was taken at a much earlier date than the picture on the opposite page. The destroyed walls and roof are still to be seen where they fell and are yet to be arranged in the neat piles, as seen on page 60.

Closer examination of the severed wall ends shows that much of the Victorian library structure was of brick, rendered over to look like stone. The surviving west wall with the rose window is of particular interest. This round window is part of the Victorian building of 1868, whereas the Romanesque windows below date from about 1080 and were originally part of Lanfranc's Great Dorter. Beyond the west wall of the library is the monastic cloister.

The standing remains of the Victorian library were later dismantled, except of course for the ancient fabric.

See CBB, Page 62   (Mr A. Moody)

This picture was taken in the south precincts and looks over the inner precincts wall towards a devastated medieval building, known as The Plumery. In the days of Christ Church Priory it was part of a school complex. Then, after the dissolution, it was allocated to stall VIII of the New Foundation of the Dean and Chapter. It saw use as a stable block and was last used as a garage, under the auspices of Canon Crum (see also page 55). The Plumery received a direct hit from a high explosive bomb on 1st June 1942. It was later partially demolished, when quantities of Elizabethan panelling recovered from the remains were put onto a bonfire. On the right of the picture can be seen the splintered trees from the Campanile area of the south precincts. Beyond is the pinnacle of St Thomas' Church in Burgate Street. In recent years a building housing public conveniences was built on the ruins of The Plumery.

(Mr A. Moody)

The Cathedral did not completely escape from the effects of the 4-ton bomb that so narrowly missed its intended target. This view of the south side of Trinity Chapel shows that many windows were blasted in and their framework dislodged. Fortunately, much of the medieval glass had been removed in 1938 and put into safe storage. On the left is St Anselm's Chapel, which was built in the early twelfth century, at the same time as Anselm's 'Glorious' Choir. It survived the devastating fire of 1174 and was later incorporated into the current replacement choir and Trinity Chapel, built by William of Sens and William the Englishman.

Amazingly enough, apart from blast damage and some minor burning to the roof of the south aisle of the nave, the main body of the Cathedral escaped unscathed.

See BOC, Page 40   (Mr A. Moody)

THE DEANERY AND NORTH PRECINCTS

The Deanery is one of the old buildings situated around the Green Court that sustained severe blast damage during the blitz of Canterbury. The old photograph comes from the archives of the Kent Messenger and features the Deanery with the damage received in both the June and October raids of 1942.

Other damaged buildings around the Green Court included the Forrens Gate and the King's School dining hall, both situated on the north side of the green.

Many of the buildings now in the hands of either the Dean and Chapter or the King's School once belonged to the extensive Benedictine Christ Church Priory. Before the dissolution, the Deanery building was known as the Prior's New Lodging. It was constructed in about 1500, during the time of Prior Goldstone II, on the site of the demolished bath house block. The large tower-like structure of flint and stone, adjoining the south side and visible on the right of both pictures, belongs to an earlier construction phase. This was built in the late 15th century, under Prior Sellinge.

The main part of the Prior's New Lodging was only about 40 years old when it was surrendered to the New Foundation of the Dean and Chapter and allocated to the first Dean, Nicholas Wotton.

The Deanery has received a number of alterations to its fabric over the years. The first occasion was in 1569, when a disastrous fire caused much damage, particularly to the roof. The more recent bomb damage of 1942, particularly during the October raid, left extensive damage to the frontage, some of which collapsed. (There had also been some bomb damage in one of the autumn raids of 1940.) Undaunted by this, the incumbent Dean, Hewlett Johnson, continued to reside in the undamaged portions of the Deanery.

(Kent Messenger)

The impressive post-war restoration of the Deanery building was carried out under the auspices of a Canterbury architect, Harold Anderson. During restoration work inside, behind a beautiful 18th century fireplace that had been blown out, was revealed the Elizabethan fireplace of the time of Archbishop 'Nosey' Parker. Behind that was the original immense medieval brick opening. Each was photographed and the work reinstated.

(Paul Crampton)

To the east of the Cathedral can be found an ancient house, known as Meister Omers. It was built in the middle of the 15th century as a guest or lodging house and was subsequently leased to various ecclesiastical and secular occupants. After 1540 and under the New Foundation, Meister Omers was allocated to Stall XI. It continued to be a canon's residence until 1936, when it was let to the King's School, who still have it.

The picture was taken from the Kent Memorial Gardens and looks towards the south-east corner of Meister Omers. Blast damage has dislodged many roof tiles and destroyed most of the windows. For a more learned architectural history of this building, including many detailed drawings, please refer to 'The Archaeology of Canterbury' volume IV, published by the Canterbury Archaeological Trust.

(Mr A. Moody)

Along the north side of the Green Court can be found an interesting range of buildings once associated with Christ Church Priory. The upper picture shows the badly blasted King's School building that was once the Priory Granary. To the left is the Forrens Gate that was extensively damaged in the June blitz. Later, the gate was completely restored so well that it is hard to believe it was ever badly damaged in the first place.

(Mr A. Moody: Courtesy Canterbury Museums)

This picture shows the blasted but surviving Kent War Memorial, built to the memory of the sons and daughters of Kent who fell in the Great War. It is, of course, the centre piece of the Memorial Gardens, to be found to the east of the Cathedral. The east end of Meister Omers can be seen in the background. In the past, this area has been a bowling green and, before that, part of a larger area known as the Old Convent Garden. Before 1540 the church of St Mary Queningate occupied part of the site and the intra-mural Queningate Lane also passed across it.

Behind the war memorial, part of the north wall of the Old Convent Garden is visible. It was built in the early 15th century of Tudor red bricks and contains a number of bee boles. These are recesses found in ancient walls to house small beehives.

(Mr A. Moody: Courtesy Canterbury Museums)

In the north-west corner of the Green Court is the famous Norman Staircase, built by Prior Wibert in 1153. It was lucky to escape any serious damage. Not so lucky was the King's School Dining Hall on the right of the picture, the west end of which was completely destroyed. It, too, was later superbly restored. The dining hall was once the Priory Brewhouse and the staircase once led to the North Hall or Aula Nova. *See BOC, Page 41 — Top* (Mr A. Moody: Courtesy Canterbury Museums)

(Above) This lovely view of the rear elevation of Christ Church Gate and the surrounding buildings in the precincts dates from August of 1942. It is hard to believe that only a few yards to the east is such a wide area of devastation. Beyond the gate are the roofs of buildings in The Parade and High Street. The tower of St Margaret's Church can also just be seen.

(Fisk-Moore)

(Below) The final study shows the Green Court to the north of the Cathedral, and the battered buildings around it. On the right is the Deanery, blasted from the June blitz, but awaiting the more serious damage to be sustained in the October 1942 blitz. On the north side of the Green Court and partially hidden by a tree is the badly damaged Forrens Gate and its associated buildings.

(Mr A. Moody: Courtesy Canterbury Museums)